This is for all the poor buggers that have had the misfortune of training me, and the poor buggers that have been trained by me.

Dedicated to my poor wife, and to the man who looks like my nan.

0

Table of Contents

Introduction

The first thing you need to know before reading this book: what Iaido is.

Iaido, pronounced ee-eye-dough (not eye-eee-dough), is a martial art that has its roots in the feudal age of Japan. It's an art where you practice kata, or pre-arranged forms or movement designed to get into your muscle memory, helping you react to attacks and situations with a Japanese sword (which is the only cool bit of Iaido).

Iaido is a sister art to Kendo, which is much better-known, but it really doesn't look much like Kendo to an outsider. Iaido is a martial art that will cause people to tip their heads like a confused Alsatian when you try to explain it.

It's hard to understand how essentially 'dancing with a sword' can be seen as a legitimate martial art, but it is. Articulating it to someone whose entire martial arts background is that they watched Bloodsport once is tricky to say the least, and the reality is that even if they do fathom what it's about, they still haven't a clue why you'd bother to dress up two or three times a week and wave a sword around when it adds little value to everyday life. It's not self-defence, so why bother? Well, for me it's same reason as people collect stamps, spot trains, dress up and go to Comic-con, or go to a pub. I enjoy it. I've been learning it for over 16 years, and I'm still really very average at it, but ultimately, I don't really care about that. It's what I like to do.

There have been other benefits from practicing Iaido. Some of the greatest friends I have are students of the art, and I'm lucky to have crossed paths with these legendary people. Don't get me wrong, like all clubs and organisations there are loads of complete wankers, arseholes, egotistical wastes of good human skins, and those that don't wash. You can put up with the odd bell-end, as the good ones really do more than make up for them.

Oddly, despite the rest of this book, being part of the Iaido world has led to me being a more tolerant and understanding person. Before Iaido I'd never met a trans-person, didn't know anyone with a different sexual orientation to me, hadn't really experienced people with Asperger's or Autism, and frankly had led a very sheltered life generally. Martial arts attract a very diverse group of humans that wouldn't normally be friends, yet it seems to mix them together like a perfect cocktail. That is something I really like. There are still plenty of spotty virgins and fantasists, but Iaido has so much more to offer than that.

This book is about my experiences of running a dojo, saturated by 'Iaido wisdom of the week' excerpts from blog I put out to all my students, picking a word or phrase they will hear in the dojo and trying to explain it in layman's terms. Also, there are other excerpts from the dojo webpage we have.

I hope you enjoy.

The dojo leader

Maybe 'Confessions of a Reluctant Sensei' would be a more accurate title for this book.

I've been running our dojo for 8 years as I write this. I had already been happily training at another club for 8 or 9 years, when life happened. I split with my ex-wife and then started going out with someone else I had met at a god-awful martial arts display in Gillingham.

The martial arts displays that I've seen in UK are not crowd pleasers. There's lots of kids showing the one karate kata they've learned, there's a really bad judo display where again it's kid carnage, only this time with screaming mothers and a few fucks thrown in. Occasionally you get a bit of synchronised Tai Chi, and Ju Jitsu clubs waving a staff like it's the first time they've picked one up, and it's not great.

The day I met my now-wife I was going to be part of the Iaido display. As usual we'd been promised a decent wood surface, and this time it was rubber mats taped together. I lined up at the front and a guy on his mobile frantically said to the person on the other end, 'mate, I got to go now, there's about to be some crazy ninja shit'. I will never know for sure what he expected to see. Was it a scene from Kill Bill? Darth Maul v Obi Wan maybe? Whatever it was the look of disappointment on his face told me for certain that Seitei Iaido kata was not what he was hoping for. He soon left. It was all I could do to not burst out laughing.

I wonder if, when people think martial arts display, they remember the All Valley under 18s karate tournament only to attend and wonder why there's no crane kicks and leg sweeping? To me, martial arts attract students that are less likely to be muscle bound gods and are instead a mash up of Manga fantasists, wannabe Jedi, and people that would look more at home at a real ale society. There are significant beards, bald heads, sagging bellies and some really boring fuckers. I'm proudly one of those, only without the beard.

Anyway, I got together with a student from a different club. I moved in with her and she generously took me and my kids on. Only a pretty special person would be willing to do that. I got lucky.

We now needed to train together at a single dojo. Her club trained afternoon on a Sunday, and mine twice during the week. Childcare meant weeknights was the only option (we had the kids every Sunday) so we asked her teacher if she could transfer to my club? Of course, in Martial Arts there is ego, there is entitlement, and there's always a problem, and her teacher said no.

Lineage is very important in Iaido. It was always taught within the family or clan, and not to people outside of that group. That made sense when your life might depend on techniques the other bloke hadn't seen, but it became much less relevant after the invention of Youtube. The upshot of this is that there is a tradition in Iaido that you don't move from one dojo to another, and in order to change you must ask your teacher to approach the other teacher. For her teacher, making this request was apparently out of the question; she wasn't going to be allowed to continue her hobby with me if it meant she would be changing dojo - the tradition was deemed more important than our situation. That's the problem with tradition. It's sometimes seen as more important than common sense.

I didn't want to put my teacher in an impossible position by asking him to take on my future wife against her current teacher's expressed wishes. This left me in a bind: train without her, or not train at all. So, in order to try and not upset my teacher I resigned from his school. I was gutted to leave, but the thing is, when a woman will give up her life for you and your kids, giving up a hobby seemed insignificant.

A month had passed and it became evident that, despite us both pretending we didn't, we both really missed training. There was only one path left open to us – we opened our own club. I had the required grade in Iaido and had completed the training course needed to open a dojo years before, so in February 2014 we found a hall, filled out the paperwork, and we picked up the keys.

Thus, the journey to teach Iaido took its first steps.

This book is about my time learning and teaching Iaido, the pitfalls of not knowing enough, the highs and lows I've encountered, and the fun and misery of it all. I'm not an expert or any kind of authority on the subject, and I don't pretend to be. What I have done here is to document my anecdotes and to be open about my experiences trying to get by in what is sometimes an awkward and difficult universe. Iaido is much bigger than a martial art alone; it's a community, a social circle, a support network and a recipe for depression all rolled into one.

I've been lucky, I've had great students around me, brilliant people to help me, and most of all the greatest Senpai you could hope for. So good, I married her.

We begin.

Iaido Clothing – the threads of the art

The Iaido Gi is a fairly thick over-jacket that is worn over a smaller thinner white jacket called a juban. They're usually long and can be very sweaty in the summer depending on the material it's made of.

This is a Juban, the under-shirt that you wear under a Gi. Useful in the winter, awful in the summer, they have holes under the arms to breathe.

Both this and the Gi are held against you with a long belt (obi).

The hakama is a pair of huge, pleated trousers that are worn down to the ankles. They are tied on by four straps that extend across the waistline and that are very difficult to untie quickly when you're desperate for a shit.

The obi is a belt that is usually several feet long, & is wrapped around you several times before being tied (unless you have the thicker Velcro version which goes round you once). The thickness of the belt supports the sword.

Tabi are socks you are allowed to wear in the dojo that make you look like you have a devil's cloven hooves, or like you're a ninja turtle. These are useful when you're training on shit floors or on cold days.

A haori is an overcoat that can be worn when it's cold, or when you fancy looking like an 80s headmaster that carries a sword. Made of similar material to the Gi, they have sleeves a wizard would be proud of.

Opening a dojo

When opening a club there's so much to think about. Finding an affordable hall, finding an affordable hall with a decent floor, finding an affordable hall with a decent floor and a high enough ceiling, finding an affordable hall with a decent floor, high enough ceiling and with availability on a night you can actually make it. These places are out there, but god you really have to go looking to find one.

This often means having to ring up a lot of churchgoing folk and explain that you're looking for a hall to hire, you're a martial artist, and although you'll be bringing a Japanese sword with you each week you are in fact not a psycho and have no plans to murder anyone, smash up the hall, or rob the Post Office.

This, I found, goes one of three ways: one, they give zero fucks, assume you're a nutter and fuck you off. Two, and this is the option I hope for; they say yes as you're sexy income to them, and ask no questions, or three, and this is the worst, they ask you a lot of questions, and these questions will be saturated by them telling you all about some friend or person they know that does or did a martial art, usually a completely different one, with them showing far too much interest or understanding when it's pretty clear they know not a thing about any of it.

I've rented 3 venues over the years. Two church halls and one nursery. One has more glitter to clear up.

The first time we went to hire a hall we did the usual pre-hire things. You go along, meet the caretaker or vicar, have a look

13

round the hall, work out just how cold you'd be in winter (church hall equals hypothermia) and how roasted you'll be in Summer (extra crispy), check the changing facilities, and by that I mean see if there's enough room in the loo to get your clobber on, and then see which parts of the hall floor are useable. These halls are often hired out for disco-based functions and as such there are often areas in front of the DJ where people have the 'erection selection' dances at the end of the evenings. These are very smooth and great for martial arts practice. Our floor had two decent areas of training, and large toilets. It was a goer.

As a side note, the KFC over the road from the hall we rented was robbed by a man with a samurai sword the week before we began training there. As omens go it was a pretty worrying one, but the chicken there is really good.

I didn't know what to call the club. I rang a 6th Dan I knew who is fluent in Japanese, and asked for an appropriate name. Eventually he came back with a name for us. He explained that part of the word meant refreshed and invigorated, which I thought was a great angle. I'm not fluent in Japanese however, so for all I know the word means 'dojo full of bell ends'. I'm hoping that's not the case.

Iaido wisdom of the week: 'Shaku'

Shaku is a Japanese measurement equivalent of 11.93 inches, 30.3 cm, or roughly half the length of my penis. Roughly.

When choosing a sword, it's important to choose the right size, and this is measured in shaku. Too short and drawing the sword becomes difficult, too long and you might not even be able to draw it at all.

As well as the length, weight is also important (though no girl ever complained it was too light). Too heavy and your arms will ache making it difficult to control, too light and it feels like you're flicking a pen about.

Finally, and possibly more important than the weight, is the balance of the sword. A heavy sword is much easier to control when balanced correctly. Poorly balanced swords are hard to control at the end of cuts, damage your joints, and actually just make your Iai look a bit shit.

On the subject of swords, when you buy one don't get anything outlandish or colourful. It can be tempting to want to be flamboyant and noticed, but it's much better to be known for your good Iai, and not for your crazy looking sword. Don't be tempted to get anything silly. Simple is classy.

How not to advertise for students

So, we had a hall, we had a deal, and we had a Tuesday night session booked every week. We had a dojo, we had a name, and things were cooking. What we didn't have was students. No problem we thought, let's go get some.

Iaido, as explained earlier, is not the best known of the martial arts. You put a poster on a notice board with 'Judo club' on it and everyone knows what that is, people notice, and the poster has done its job. I don't know why, but looking back this didn't occur to me. We put a local poster campaign out with a silhouette of a samurai on it, saying Iaido, the venue, time, and date. This unsurprisingly brought no people whatsoever to the club. I don't know why I thought it would. The two most successful posters we had were placed in the reception of the church hall, and in a very well-known local supermarket notice board. The one at the hall collected dust, the one at the supermarket was torn down mere hours after we put it up.

Our dojo was registered at the governing body's web page, and this brought a little more interest.

What I hadn't done on that web page is explain that if you were interested, to get in touch prior to coming along.

One really very hot summer night my then girlfriend (now wife) and I were training when two guys in their twenties turned up to try out the club. No problem I thought, I had a couple of wooden swords I'll just give them one each and give them a beginner lesson they'll never forget. So, I lined them up and away we went.

Throughout the whole lesson the two guys seemed quite uncomfortable. They seemed nice, but I noticed they kept looking at each other quite disturbed. I couldn't quite place what was wrong, but I continued on. At the end of the lesson, I thanked them, and they left promptly. It was only then I realised that, because it was hot, and because it was only myself and girlfriend going to be training that I didn't bother with a gi (the overcoat part of the uniform) and instead had only put the juban (a white, short shirt) on, and the hakama (pleated trousers). These were too big, the shirt much too short, and the result was that my naked thighs were exposed the whole way through training, and it was like the guys had turned up at some really weird martial art where you covered up completely, except for your milky thighs. Unsurprisingly, they never returned.

I was planning to propose to my girlfriend that night and even had the engagement ring in my sword oil box, but that had to go out the window because these guys had turned up. I should be grateful for that. No one should propose in the Iaido equivalent of arseless chaps. I did propose the next day and I did remember to wear trousers.

Next, I made us a website. There are people that design websites for a living and make good money doing it, so looking back I'm again surprised that my attitude to this was that it would be a total piece of piss and soon we'd be winning awards for our design and ambitious achievement. Looking back at the first version of the website I can see that it was really awful. Very wordy with lots of pictures that made little sense. Fortunately, there's a way of gauging how good your website is, and that's students walking through the door, or a lack thereof. So, I changed the website to a slightly, and really do mean slightly less shit website. Still brimming with terrible ideas and content, but mildly less wordy. I now have an appreciation for every website I go on, and the decisions that went into it.

I've tried all sorts of ways of getting us out there. I registered on Yell (the online yellow pages) and put us under martial arts. If you happen to use Yell instead of Google, then you'll certainly find us about 6th down the list if you look for Martial arts in the area. Sad thing is that is that nobody uses Yell when Google is available, except maybe someone's Gran. Somewhere.

I registered in a local area physical education website that tells people what is available in the area. Let's face it though, Iaido is a niche market compared with other things that are out there. Who'd pick it when there's kick-boxing or badminton available?

've never had a single student enquiry from these methods. What I have had is maybe a hundred sales calls as a result, usually from people telling me that if I advertise through them, for a fee, they could make my 'business' massive in no time, and I could have thousands of paying students. Where would I put them all? There's only room for about 8 in the erection selection areas of the floor.

The best form of advertising I've found is getting noticed by other Japanese martial art dojos in the area. There's often students that want to try more than martial art as it means less time at home with the other half and the kids, which let's face it, can't be bad. That was our jumping-off point.

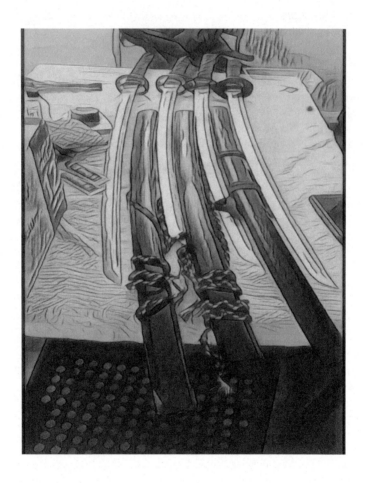

Iaido wisdom of the week: 'Depth of practice'

What is depth of practice, and how is it shown or relevant to Iaido?

This is not always the easiest question to answer. Especially when different teachers are looking for different emphasis on different techniques. Ultimately, I try think about it like this:

Basic level: *Try to look like you've done it before, and that it's not all new.*

For example, a beginner can take Seiza (sitting on your knees) competently in that they can probably clear their hakama and sit down. When you have more experience you can take it under caution, more quietly, whilst concentrating fully on an opponent and maintaining calm. Therefore, showing your depth of practice.

Next level: *Show what you know.*

Not making mistakes, deliver uniform cuts at the correct height, and show you understand concepts beyond the basics of footwork and directions. A certain competence in the presentation of your kata. Showing you know much more than a beginner by delivering consistent, better movement than you'd see a beginner do.

Top level: *No fucking clue.*

Don't know as I'm not even close to that level! I'm told small movements and nuances make all the difference in identifying depth of practice. A breath

20

on a cut or a small movement of the eyes can identify a more senior level during a form. Basically, apply what you know to every form, and think about the opponent or opponents too. There's so much to learn and practice, so keep going. Your knowledge will start to show through your Iai as you begin to succeed.

Wake up! You fell asleep. Breakfast ready.

My unfair categorisation of students

I know that labelling students, or anyone for that matter, can be a really bad thing, but when a new face walks through the door they tend to mainly fit into one of the following categories:

1. Mid-life Crisis Black-Belt
2. Broken Warrior
3. Young Virgin Male
4. Potential Post Office Robber
5. Manga Twat
6. Missing Females and Other Genders
7. The Goldfish

The good news is the category doesn't define you forever, and if you stay at training, you'll likely move from one to another, hopefully avoiding being a Cat 4.

All students are always readily accepted, except category 4s. Why you start is not why you continue.

I will admit that I was a *Mid-life Crisis Black Belt* when I started. I wanted a black belt so that I could tell all my friends about it, unaware at the time that: 1) It's not impressive to have one in the slightest, and 2) That they could not give less of a fuck about me getting a black belt in a martial art they've never heard of, and once they had checked out on YouTube they gave even less of a fuck, if that's possible. I think psychologically it's because when I was a kid I was mad on Judo, and was pretty decent, but gave up before getting that holy grail of martial art prizes, the 'black belt', and I wanted to rectify this.

I've been Dan graded for years now, and I think I've moved on to being a **Broken Warrior**, and this is for me the most common student you tend to find learning Iaido. It's a person, usually over 40, that has had success in other martial arts that wants to continue to enjoy that world despite having a bad back and dodgy belly. In my dojo alone we have had Aikido students who struggle to walk easily, a Kyoku Shin Karate student (that also learns Ju Jitsu) with toes that can't bend as they've been broken so many times, and others will all sorts of physical issues caused from years of training. Yet every lesson they drag themselves through the door, get changed and give it their all. It's to be commended. And occasionally laughed at.

Occasionally a **Young Virgin Male** will join the club. Always in their twenties, always in much better physical health than anyone else there, and always a brilliant student. Each one we have had has been a pleasure to teach, and you cannot believe that a person of that calibre has managed to find their way to our little club.

The sad thing is, there's a problem with Young Virgin Males. You know they are capable of becoming an Iaido success if they continue to train and work damn hard, but there is a really big roadblock. They have testicles; really big testicles, throbbing, full of Harry Monk, and as soon as they find someone that will play with their dingle-dangle they'll be gone quicker than you imagine, and then they become a very different swordsman, one that will be spending more time in someone else than in your dojo.

23

Ironically, I think that trying a martial art gives them that little bit of lacking confidence, makes them feel more interesting, and bridges the gap from them being a serial masturbator to a genuine lover of the ladies (loving other men is OK too, of course). It's a catch 22 situation (that's not an STD). Really though, it's a good thing, and I've enjoyed watching every Young Virgin Male move on to someone better. Not literally. I've not filmed them or anything.

Iaido is just a hobby at the end of the day, and some things are just more important. One of our students was in his late 20s when he lost his virginity. He told us and we gave him a round of applause and a pat on the back. Seriously though, this was really big for him.

Sometimes on very long journeys together you get to know your students in a lot of detail, and this particular student opened up about it never happening for him, even though he wanted it to. He'd meet a girl he liked, and his confidence would dissolve and each time it happened it felt worse. Like all your friends you look out for students, and it wasn't nice to hear that he had this anxiety, so when he finally did the dirty deed it was actually quite a relief. The path of dating did seem to be a struggle for him in the weeks after. He asked us where he should take her for a meal, and we suggested anywhere but Nandos. So, he took her to Nandos. He explained he was going to take her to look at racing cars. I asked if she likes racing cars? He said no, but he did, so shouldn't he enjoy it? Anyway, he came into the dojo a few weeks later to say he was single again, which was a good thing as it was really interfering with his X Box time. Sometimes I despair.

Potential Post Office Robbers are the most worrying, and fortunately the rarest of the student types. It's not that they will actually rob a post office (largely because there's so few post offices now, they're not up for the travelling), but that you wouldn't trust them to not do something stupid with a sword when not training. At best they'll cut their garden weeds down by swinging it about in the back yard, and possibly take a limb off, and at worst you'd see a mug shot of them on the 6 o'clock news.

I was in a class once when a guy turned up and showing everyone his razor-sharp samurai sword that he just happened to have at home, and thought he'd bring it to training. He told us how he'd definitely kill burglars with it, and possibly his neighbour he disliked. He had a slightly frightening laugh that was a bit maniacal and was mumbling away to himself throughout training. When trying to explain the basics he really wasn't listening.

The solution was simple. He was given a wooden sword and asked to practice one movement, a blood shake (literally where you flick the sword to get the blood off) the whole 2-hour lesson. You could see he couldn't handle the repetition and he never came back. I don't think we were the right school for him. I was relieved.

In the last few years there's been a different kind of person looking us up. An equal split of males and females who I will categorise as **Manga Twats**. Fantasists are big fans of swords.

They like them in anime, Star Wars, Game of Thrones, and whole host of other shows. They like them so much that they like to dress up like them, or mash up the costumes together, and they like pictures of themselves doing this. A lot of pictures. This is fine, whatever floats your boat is good as long as you're not bothering others, until they turn up at your dojo wanting to learn a martial art, but actually what they really want it pictures of themselves in Japanese clobber, looking 'cool' with swords.

I once had a new student ring up asking to come along. No problem, I said. He said he already owned the gear from learning Kenjutsu, a similar martial art, so I said great, see you then. When he turned up, he was dressed as an anime Samurai, chest out with a huge red bow on his waist. He then showed me the nunchakus he'd made out of a windowsill (I'm not making this up). He lasted one session.

I've had a woman call me and ask if her daughter could come to train as she got a plastic light sabre for Christmas and they were fed up with her twirling it round at home, so would she be able to come to ours and do it there instead? When I explained the repetition and how long it would be before they could actually use a sword, they asked me if her daughter could use a lightsabre instead? No. No, she couldn't.

One person sent me an email and explained they were into anime, and could they come along and see that we do. I said yes, they were welcome to come and give it a try. They then emailed to say they'd had a panic attack about the possibility of coming, so they'd changed their mind, but might come along and get some pictures if they felt up to it another time. Lucky us.

26

I didn't grow up in the Instagram age and can go quite a long time before taking a picture of myself, so I do struggle to understand the modern world idea of constantly showing yourself off on public access websites. There are definite benefits to having people do this though. It's only through people taking endless pictures of their terrible dinners that I've discovered I'm a half decent cook, and for that I'm grateful. Having people approach your club though with their sole intention of showing the world how cool they look with a sword is very much not cool. If you want to learn a martial art leave the bloody camera at home and bring a good learning attitude with you instead. Don't they already have clubs for cosplay already? Why do they need mine too?

Swords are the attraction of Iaido unless you happen to be into seriously baggy trousers (the hakama is a trouser that MC Hammer would definitely have been attracted to). I too was enamoured with the idea of owning one when I started. They can be a very beautifully crafted tool, but really that's all that they are: a tool. A decorative and shiny tool for killing, but a tool none the less. For me that awesome feeling of owning a sword lasting about a month (meaning I'm a tiny part Manga Twat, I hadn't thought of that before. Self-loathing just increased). After explaining to my mother (who I must stress I had not lived with for 10 years, and I was nearly 30) that I had taken up a hobby that required me to own a sword she did the thing that any other mother would 'obviously' do and rang the authorities to tell them I had a sword. Turns out they weren't interested. Also turns out my mother is an arsehole, but sadly I was already aware of this.

The next category, **Missing Females and Other Genders,** is named that way as we've had no females actually try Iaido at our club. Well, OK, other than the one I'm married to, but as we started this venture together and she has more black belts than the men's section of M & S, I'm grouping her with Broken Warriors. We do get enquires, and I say please come along, and I try to be welcoming. They just never have made it to an actual practice. Each time there's been a last-minute cancellation and piss-poor reason given which really sounds like a bad excuse to me, or they've simply not bothered.

In martial arts there are more males than females generally. As a student of mine (a Young Virgin Male) once stated loudly at his first Iaido event, 'fuck me, this is a sausage fest'. I don't know why Iai doesn't attract more females though, I really don't. The women I know at other dojos all really enjoy it and do really well, but they are heavily outnumbered. Iaido is basically wall-to-wall chaps.

We haven't had other genders approach us either, and maybe they, like the women, just have something better to do with their lives. It's actually a shame though. It's a martial art where gender, weight, strength, and all of those things that segregate people in sports don't apply at all. Everyone is grouped in together, and competitions are only divided by grades of the students, nothing else. It really is inclusive to everyone, which can only be a good thing. It's very modern and inclusive for something very traditional. I do hope at some point a woman walks through the door, just so the YVMs can actually meet one, so they realise there's more than just my wife alive in this world.

It would give them so much hope, and something new to masturbate over.

Finally, there's the *Goldfish* category. There are some students that join the club and pick up information really easily. You say it once, they get it, and they work on improving their technique with that knowledge safety tucked away in their brains. They can't necessarily apply that information, but it's remembered. And then we have the Goldfish. For these people every single lesson is like their first lesson, every technique brand new to them, even if you've shown it to them 20 times before. You show them time after time after time, and just hope that one day the penny will drop. I do worry that when this happens the sky may fall in, the apocalypse will happen, and the dead will walk again. No immediate danger though.

Iaido wisdom of the week: 'Shatner's cortex'

It's the part of the brain that controls over acting which can make your kata look hammy.

Okay, so it's not 'Shatner's cortex', I don't know what the actual word is for this but try and keep your face neutral when you are doing kata. There's nothing worse than angry poo faces when you are doing Iaido.

Picture it. You're doing the Iai of your life in a national final. You turn to face your opponent, ready to end their life, and the judges don't see your impeccable cut, all they see is your red face, reminding them of a time when they did a difficult poo themselves. You don't need that.

The danger of a sword is not understanding people

Scaring people sells newspapers and advertising space, and what could be scarier than a nutter with a sword? One poor disturbed bloke attacks someone with a 'samurai sword' and the papers, rather than campaigning for better mental health services, are screaming that there is an Imminent Threat To Us All and the only solution is to ban swords and knives.

The only problem is that a sword isn't dangerous, it's the person holding it. Take away the sword and the attacker will decide to use whatever else is available. For example, a Stanley knife, a hammer, a piece of 4 by 2, and a wrench can all kill or harm you just as well as a sword. They're far more readily available, easier to use, and are far cheaper than a sword. What are we going to do about that? Ban DIY stores?

As a result of newspaper campaigns, there are strict legal limitations on owning blunt swords in the UK, and somewhat fewer limitations on owning sharp ones. And no, that doesn't make sense. As I'm sure you can imagine, this is somewhat vexing for students of Iaido. Learning the art (and I can't over emphasise that word: it's an art) of drawing the sword is not really possible without one. Substitute it with something else and it's no longer the art of drawing a sword. It's the art of drawing the plastic kid's toy, or whatever.

Every dojo leader I know would never let a student move on from a wooden sword to a training blade (and that's a blunted sword by the way, not even a razor sharp one) if they had any morsel of doubt in their mind that the person lacked the maturity to handle the concept that the sword is for use in training and nothing else.

Before I leave, my sword, like every other person's in the dojo, is tied into the scabbard, then placed in a sword bag, which is tied up, then placed into another carrying case, and zipped up. If I was attacked on the way to practice and I was carrying it, I think I'd be ready for combat in a little over 2 minutes by time I'd fucked about getting the knots loosened. Every person I know who trains with a sword follows the same practice.

Fortunately, the police in the UK seem to be very sensible about this. For example, a friend of mine was on a train coming home from practice when officers approached him and asked him what was in his bags? He explained that he had his kit in one bag, and in the other was a sword as he was coming home from training, and they said, 'no problem' and moved on to someone else. I've heard many other positive stories about the police from others too.

I once was with three students on the way back from a training seminar in London when we stopped at the O2 Arena for an impromptu meal. Most of us had arranged the swords to go directly back with other students, but one of our group, not realising we were going for meal, still had her sword bag with her.

We took the cable car over the Thames to the Arena, and my mind was completely occupied by the fact that I was in agony; as I'd had several pints and I was desperate for the toilet. This is probably why I hadn't worried too much about her having the weapon in her bag, I was more worried I would soak my shorts. There was real danger that day.

As we walked into the Arena, a security guard approached us and asked what was in the bag? Not a surprise in hindsight, as sword bags are an unusual shape and it would have been very conspicuous. The lady, without any hesitation announced that it was a samurai sword. The security guard, who clearly didn't believe her candour, asked if he could take it and run it through the scanner. She agreed and we stood there and watched the bag go on a conveyor belt, and on the screen above was a perfect silhouette of a Samurai sword. The security guard now looking very confused as to why a woman was wondering around the O2 Arena with a Samurai sword, and explained where she'd been, and he explained that (quite reasonably) she couldn't take it in. No problem. He agreed to return the sword to her after the meal and keep it safe. So, we had a great meal, came out and collected the sword. There is a dark side to this though. I do wonder if the reaction by security would have been the same had it not have been a white 60 year old woman bringing in a sword, and instead had been a person from a different demographic, but I guess we'll never know.

Public fear is something that the media love to use to whip up sales and it's very disappointing that supplementing their finances is more important than reporting reality.

If I want to buy a sword from a martial arts supplier in the UK, it's not an easy thing to do; they don't just give them away. They want membership numbers and proof of why I need it for, then I must provide I.D. and lastly a shit load of money. They're not cheap. A reasonable and decent Iaito, which is a blunted sword built well enough to practice with, starts at nearly £300.

Razor sharp swords called 'shinken' can do real damage, but are usually hand made and are much more expensive. You can buy sharp replica swords quite cheaply, but they're designed for displaying in a room, not to actually use or train with. These 'wall-hangers' are liable to break just waving them about and are mostly a danger is to the person trying to use one.

Iaido wisdom of the week: Kensen

Pressuring, specifically from the tip of the sword.

Think about Chuden-no-kamae – you are aiming your sword at the opponent's throat, rather than over his head. It's far more threatening and makes sure you are a comfortable distance from your opponent.

Think about someone pointing a gun at you. Is he pointing it at your throat? Not so good. Three feet above your head? Not so bad.

Iaido wisdom of the week: Merihari

Refers to the overall pace of the kata, the way that some parts quicken, and others relax and slow down. Basically, it's the change in movement that stops the kata being mechanical and jerky.

Of course, Merihari is not to be confused with Mary Berry. One is a Japanese term described above, and the other is a lady that makes fabulous baked goods. Try not to confuse them.

The conspicuous walk

A long time ago a younger, slimmer, more energetic, and far less grey version of me was looking for a martial art to try. As I said in an earlier chapter, I practiced Judo when I was a kid and really loved it (until cars, girls and alcohol became far more interesting) and I wanted something that would give me a similar buzz.

There are a lot of available types of martial art out there and knowing what would be good idea and what would be a bad idea is very difficult. For example, what makes a martial arts establishment a good place to train at? Should the dojo be part of an official governing body or global organisation (and if they're not, would they tell you?)? Is it about the syllabus and expectations of you? Is it about the quality of the venue itself and the environment? Is it the actual art that is best suited to you? Is the dojo leader a good teacher of the art? Is the dojo leader well versed and practiced in that art, and also respected? Is it financially okay, or are you being ripped off? So much to think about.

I started off by ringing around the local clubs. Half of them no longer existed but hadn't taken the phone numbers off of the internet. That was irritating. The ones that were open mostly had different sessions to what was on their websites, and some hadn't put anything about which grades were allowed to attend what days. It was a mess. Ultimately the search led to a Kendo dojo locally to me, and thought 'why not, let's give it a go'.

I made the conspicuous walk into the sports centre where the club was. Naturally you always feel a dickhead walking into a place where there are lots of people that don't know you, and you're waiting to be judged by them.

The teacher was, even on first impressions, a really weird guy. When I introduced myself, he acknowledged me with what seemed like obvious suspicion and distance. Not a warm welcome and instead more of a mild interrogation. I answered honestly all the questions and he nodded and sighed in equal measure. I was unpleasantly surprised, given the size of the sports centre, that we were crammed into a Squash court.

I stood in the corner like a spare prick at a wedding whilst the other students unpacked their bags and unwrapped their shinai (a bamboo sword used for kendo). The teacher gave me my first shinai which I had paid up front for, and then bollocked me for holding it incorrectly as he passed it to me (must have missed the part about holding a shinai in P.E. at school).

I was then lined up and told to follow on with everyone else. A number of cutting exercises with the shinai then followed. This I could follow just fine, except all of the other students were shouting something each time they cut, and I really couldn't place what they were yelling. Following on vaguely by waving some bamboo around I could do. Making noises at the same time, which to me at the time sounded somewhat similar to Vic Reeves mimicking a lounge singer, I really couldn't do easily. No explanation followed any of this.

The lesson went on, and cuts were put together with movements, but again without much explanation for what they were for. What I lacked in understanding I more than made up for in a workout. I

37

was completely knackered at the end. It was a physical class. After training I was invited to the apparent ritual of going over the road to the pub, and the other students all seemed really enthusiastic about this part. Not wanting to disappoint on day one I thought I should go and make an effort.

The pub was dog shit, a drinker's pub that hadn't been renovated, redesigned, or even cleaned since the 1970s. The Axminister carpet reeked of stale beer, the dark wood furniture was scored until the light wood underneath was visible in places, the obese landlord was just years from the grave, and there were crisp packets and beer mats on the floor. We sat on a large table, and I brought the drinks over. It became very apparent at this point that the teacher was the high priest, and the students his disciples, and he was going to preach to them, and they would be listening attentively. I sat there and listened as he explained his world views to the students completely unquestioned, no matter how ridiculous or insane the things he said. They laughed when they were meant to and nodded in agreement when required.

I became very uncomfortable with this. He started to talk about other Kendo clubs and people and openly berated them with a clear venom. There was obviously some back story, and I didn't know it, but the evening was hardly the uplifting and warm club experience I was hoping for.

When I got home, I looked back on the experience and realised that I'd enjoyed the physical elements of the evening, but the club and leader weren't really what I had hoped. Still, I thought it may be a one-off, so I returned twice more and each time the experience was worse. I decided to research Kendo online and found that the club I was attending wasn't part of a governing body (which means no insurance), and the teacher was very against the governing body, having been part of it before either disgracing himself or pissing them off, or something similar. It also turned out he wasn't well liked by others that practiced in the UK. The alarm bells were ringing, and it was time to try something else.

Kendo is a popular enough pastime in the UK that there are clubs all over the shop and there are usually several close enough to travel to. Except where I lived. At the time the local motorway was being dug up for three years which meant travel to and from the London area was long and arduous, and there was no easy way to get to a dojo. I went on a Kendo forum and asked where the nearest dojos were, hoping to find something more local. A person (who I'm now good mates with now all these years later) suggested I try Iaido instead as there was loads of it local to me and suggested three dojos to contact.

I rang the first one, and the person at the other end seemed to have breathing problems. They described to me what Iai was whilst doing their best Darth Vader impersonation, and didn't seem too bothered about me coming along, so I thought I'd try the second.

The second person answered the phone and I explained I was looking for a dojo. What followed was the most enthusiastic and upbeat response to any enquiry you could hope for. I didn't know what Iaido was particularly. I'd never seen it before and the descriptions I'd had were pretty vague, yet three minutes into talking to this guy and I wanted to go straight out and buy all the fucking gear there and then. He was so passionate and invested in whatever this martial art was that I really I wanted to get to the first class and watch some, and he wanted me to! This was much more like it. He not only sounded like a martial arts teacher, he sounded like an actual human being that you wouldn't mind speaking to more.

The first class I attended was purely to watch and meet the teacher. I knocked on the door and was welcomed in and seated by the door so I could watch the class. The hall was big and bright and modern, and the students all said hello when coming in before taking their positions. Prior to the class starting there was some light conversation between everyone, and a few laughs before a formal class began. Even though the teacher was in control he was fine with questions and even the odd bit of banter and frivolity. Everyone seemed happy and to be working hard. I found it a fascinating martial art to watch. It honestly looked incredibly easy and simple, so much so in fact that I couldn't really get why it couldn't be learned without any problem whatsoever. I thought it looked like a complete piece of piss.

I chatted to the teacher and some of the students afterwards. All nice people, no one berating anyone, and it gave me a good feeling that it was a place I'd like to come, although it wouldn't be for long, as after one whole session looking at it, I thought I'd be a 10th Dan Grandmaster motherfucker in no time at all, as Iai clearly was a doddle. Little did I know… Many years later I'm still striving to not be completely shit at it.

This dojo became my home from home for many years, and I loved it. Each lesson became an opportunity to switch off from the daily grind and concentrate purely on something else. I would come in, change, join the end of the line, clear my mind (of the wankers at work, my total arsehole of a boss, financial hassles, shopping lists, noisy children, that weird lump on my head that was worrying me, what the knocking noise was on the car etc) and melt into a world where all there was is the need to perfect a movement, or a cut, or learn a phrase or concept. It was incredibly liberating and a feeling that I love to this day, and I thoroughly recommend it.

Iaido has always been more to me than an obscure martial art you do in huge trousers, it's a rare way of closing the door on your life for 120 minutes.

The first month of you training will always include the feeling of the conspicuous walk, but each time it gets easier. Eventually it goes. Then a new student will come along, and it will be their turn and you're no longer the newbie.

Your job is to always remember what it was like, and to try not to make it worse for them, even if they are a fucking Manga Twat.

Iaido words of wisdom: 'Jo-Ha-Kyu'

This is an organising principle which has been taught to me as meaning "slow, medium, fast" or "beginning, middle, end."

I think of it as a rising in which the movement is getting stronger before coming to a big finish, like a tune getting louder and more intense before the crescendo.

In the dojo you've probably heard me say this phrase a few times, and almost sing it at you when you're moving in between cuts and when cutting. The singing bit is unnecessary, so apologies for that.

The kata can be divided up into different sections, each which have this 'rising action' within each movement. It's what stops your Iai looking rigid.

"Rising action" (giggles like a school boy)….

"Rigid:…. Smirks to self.

The dojo awakens

There are times in a dojo leader's life when there are definite spikes in interest in a club that involves waving swords about. The first time I noticed this was when the film '47 Ronin' came out.

For those lucky enough not to have seen it, 47 Ronin stars universally loved Keanu Reeves, and it has a generous score of 6.3 on the IMDB.

I'm certainly no connoisseur of films, and definitely not of Samurai films, but 47 Ronin may be one of the three worst films I've ever seen (along with 'Gigli' and 'Attack of the Killer Tomatoes'). Even Keanu cannot save it from being a worse experience than running a cheese grater over your helmet.

Why that film would inspire anyone to go online and look for a dojo is beyond me. Why anyone would do anything other than take the DVD back to the shop and instead spend the money more wisely is also beyond me. It came out in 2012 so DVDs were still a thing then, weren't they?

A lot of Iaido students are naturally fans of Samurai films. I've watched very few of them if I'm honest, but what I've seen I've enjoyed. Even 'The last Samurai' with Tom Cruise is pretty damn good, except the scene where he basically seems to use the force to defeat 4 or 5 attackers whilst unarmed, having spent a few months in Japan sobering up with the Samurai.

Speaking of the force, the week the trailer for the 93rd instalment of marketing giant 'Star Wars' was shown, I had three or four enquires. Coincidence? All the talk of Kylo Ren's lightsabre seemed to juice up the interest of the local community looking to do something with a sword too.

I love Star Wars. I was born in the 1970s and Star Wars toys were the greatest thing. When my Nan bought be the Millennium Falcon in 1982 it may have been the best Christmas ever, so I do understand that a film can have a real influence on a person, and that you can be deeply passionate about it. Jedi are loosely based on Samurai, so I suppose there's a link also. I've never really understood why people think the Jedi are cool. Yes, they have laser swords and dance around waving them like a majorette on speed, but they're essentially monks who aren't supposed to let anyone have any fun playing with their dingle dangles. That doesn't seem very cool to me at all. Who'd want that lifestyle? I'd rather replace using my lightsabre with using my meatsabre any day of the week,

Speaking of Samurai swords in films, Highlander always cracks me up. Don't get me wrong, it's a brilliantly entertaining romp of a movie, and the bit where Heather ages whilst Connor doesn't to Queen's 'Who wants to live forever' is moving in a way that films have forgotten to move you, but the film does have a 'couple' of flaws. For example, the sword Connor McLeod uses is supposed to wow the audience, but instead looks like a plastic kids' toy. That's trumped by the Kurgan's sword, which he keeps in a briefcase, and he then clips together like an Ikea coffee table. You almost expect him to throw away the packet of screws he didn't need after making it. My favourite scene though is where Edinburgh born and raised Sean Connery sits in a rowboat with French Christopher Lambert, and Connery asks Lambert what

Haggis is? It's absolutely fucking mental! I did read recently it's being rebooted or reinvented or something. That's got to be good for a few students, hasn't it?

Iaido wisdom of the week:

'Ki Ken Tai no Ichi'.

Basically, this is mind, sword and body as one. In other words when you attack your opponent you do so with these three ingredients all together.

In Kendo it is the combination of a Kiai (shout) whilst placing your foot and striking the intended part of the opponent together. If one part it is missing, for example you forget to Kiai, or your foot is not timed with the strike, then Ki Ken Tai no Ichi didn't happen, and if the ref saw it then it's no score. And they'd probably be laughing at you internally. Okay, there's no evidence of that, but let's face it, they probably are.

Iaido is a little different as we don't Kiai, (although I do shout internally, usually at myself when I fuck something up during a kata) but the basic is the same. Your cut should be decisive as well as your intention to cut, along with the placement of your foot just prior to the cut landing on the opponent. Your attack should be coming from your tanden (core).

Throughout each kata, try to perfect your timing so that your foot lands just, and only just, before your cut. There's nothing uglier than a step towards an opponent finishing and a clear second later a cut being launched. It just makes it look like the opponent stood there and begged for a cut to the head. Which would be pretty unusual, unless they'd been listening to Adele, in which case it's possible.

The grading weekend

Periodically in a martial art there is an opportunity to take a grading of some kind. As you'd expect it's a confirmation that you've reached a certain standard, or if you fail it's a confirmation that you didn't perform to that standard on the day, or worse you really aren't there yet. It can be rewarding or frustrating in equal measures, and I've experienced both. Also, on top of the emotional experiences it can be a very expensive business too.

The high of passing the exam is a pretty special feeling, especially if you really have put in the hours and work. Failing the test can have serious repercussions for the student. Some, and I think the minority, take it very much in their stride, take it again another time and then eventually pass. These people seem so laid back by the whole thing. I'm actually envious when I see someone like it, but it's rare. Others fail the test and go back to the dojo and hit their training harder than ever, taking into account any feedback they were given, and next time they take the test they're so much better than they were. That is the attitude that you like to see. The failure fires them up and motivates them.

The sad thing is though that a lot of people walk away from the art after failing a grading. After the announcement is made of who passed and who failed you can hear people quite loudly moaning that it's bullshit that they didn't pass, and they were much better than someone who did. I've seen people storm off never to be seen again. I've seen people crying in the carpark.

I'd be lying if I said I felt the grading standard was always fair, I think you can make a good case with strong evidence that it isn't, and people have passed that shouldn't have, and people have failed when others have passed, and I can believe it eats at you. It's difficult when I've not been in that position of failing when I should have passed to say how you should react. I failed a grading because I was crap, and I mean really crap, on the day. A few days after the test when things had settled down and I could re-live the day in my mind I realised that adrenaline have taken control and I had rushed the whole thing just to get it over with. It's hard to demonstrate your standard when you are desperately wanting it to be over. Lesson learned. I slow down now to compensate, but sometimes you have to make a mistake to learn the lesson. The important thing though is that you learn the lesson.

Walking away from the art because you fail a test is saying you didn't learn anything. That's another lesson I learned, from a completely different grading was when I took my green belt test in Judo at 12 years old. I had somehow managed to throw my much taller opponent for a measly koka (3 points, not sure they even score 3 points in Judo anymore) and whilst holding him down in a rather spurious position he farted into my mouth, and I took the whole of his sweat fart into my throat, tasting the lot. I managed to finish the hold down for the win, before coming off court and being sick. Soon after that I learned to hold my breath for hold downs where the head was 'down south'.

The current experience for my students though is something like this.

The governing body for Iaido requires you to complete a ridiculously easy exam paper weeks before the grading (honestly it's pointless, you can go on the web and get the answers if you don't know them instantly, and there's no penalty) then there's the actual test itself which usually at a seminar on a weekend of practice, when on the afternoon of the second day you go out and complete an 'embu' which is essentially five kata sandwiched between some etiquette with the sword.

The whole event usually starts after work on a Friday, when I drive around picking up the students, then the road trip begins. On the way to the services everyone is usually quite spritely and upbeat, and banter and anecdotes are welcome. In the services, inevitably a MacDonald's is sucked down before the last leg of the journey is completed far more sedately. Everyone has been at work for the day and is overtired and they just want the endless motorway driving to be over.

Between Iaido and other hobbies I have I've spent a ridiculous amount of my life in hotels, and in my experience the worst hotels in the UK are all in Birmingham. Unfortunately, my favourite of the Iaido seminars are the ones I've attended are also in Birmingham. One time we arrived at a hotel there, got our keys and went to the room. It stunk of cigarette smoke, so I went back to the counter and asked for another, which they didn't want to give me. After I got lairy and I insisted they did, and we went up to the room, but the key card didn't open the room, so back down to the counter (3 floors) and they came up with an alternative key. They had trouble but it opened, so they said if you're going out for the evening then they'll sort the lock out whilst we're away. We were going for a curry with some of the other students, so we said yes, no problem. Off we went and had a terrible meal (terrible meals at these training events are common, as everyone chooses a cheap venue to accommodate everyone, and the food is often exceedingly ropey) and several beers. When we returned there was a person waiting for us. Turns out they couldn't get back into the room as the lock was completely fucked (their words) and they said they couldn't kick the door in as it was nearly midnight, and it would freak out the other guests. We had to stay in the only room that was available, a room next to the road where they were completing an all-night re-surfacing, without any of our bags. I'll be honest, I didn't get much sleep that night. The next day I wandered down to the counter, was given my bags, given the room for free, and I was given the rooms for free for me and all the other students of mine staying there. That was how bad they realised the experience was.

On the flipside of this I've stayed in some amazing hotels and venues. I once stayed in a converted barn-house in Barnstaple in a farm, where each night we ate like kings. First night was venison pie made from their own deer, and the next was grouse wrapped with bacon, and their home-grown veg. Sure, contrasted with the usual Subway lunch or Tesco sandwiches. It was also the most picturesque place I'd ever stayed; lush green fields and hills, brushed with snow, with animals wandering about the site. You just don't get all of that with a Travelodge. Or a bath.

Anyway, you get to the hotel, check in your bags and then hit the bar. There are usually other students from around the country staying at the same hotel, so 'just a beer before bed' often turns into a proper session with people you haven't seen in a while. It's rare to actually get a good night sleep after. One time I was trying to sleep whilst a lady in the room next door decided to have some very loud (and we thought solo) 'happy time'. That keeps you awake. I've never been more pleased for someone to come so I could get some Zs.

The next day you get up, eat something that definitely won't give you the shits and head to wherever training is at. These are usually at school sports facilities that have been rented for the weekend, or at the 'cheaper end' of leisure centres or sports halls. When I say cheaper end, I mean that they often feature changing facilities with broken toilets, and they smell of sewage. One particular venue, upon flushing the one toilet that worked (door was hanging off though) shit actually started seeping through the floor. You get changed, usually in silence and head out into the sports hall. In Summer it's a million degrees and in Winter it's frozen cold. You then stand around for absolutely ages whilst the teachers get organised, then away you go. A day of training and standing about begins.

At the end you limp back to the hotel and get in the bath (if you have one in the room that is, and if you haven't you seriously regret not booking a room with one), never wanting to get out. Then it's out for the shit meal with the other students. I was in an all-you-can-eat Chinese once when a guy had put both main and pudding on the same plate because they were in the same cabinet, and you really couldn't tell them apart. That's the level of quality we're talking about (and unlike breakfast, this does guarantee the shits).

This is actually though one of the real appeals of these training days; meeting new people. You get chatting to people from all walks of life. Martial arts appeal to so many different types of people and you get a room full of people that ordinarily would never break bread together. At a single table you can get a plumber, a banker, a doctor, a bin man, a lorry driver, an engineer, and a retired former teacher all chatting away finding common ground. It really is wonderful. Of course, not everyone is a nice person, but the detestable are far outnumbered by the good company, and if you rush to the table on entry, you can pretty much monopolise a table, meaning the twats get kept away. You say goodbye three hours later than you thought you'd leave, stumble back to the hotel and try to sober up.

The next morning, moving like an old man with rickets, you head back to the venue, finish the morning training session very carefully, stretching and keeping your body as ready as possible, then break for lunch, and then the actual grading will start shortly after.

These are, of course, nerve racking for the student. Prepare all you like: it's still going to give you butterflies, because you care. Of course you care, otherwise you wouldn't be there. Some handle it better than others, and experience definitely helps, but it's always a gamble. The good news is with Iaido it's a fairly quick process. I've heard rumours of dojo and clubs of other martial arts doing all sorts of crazy things to complete a grading, such as having to bring other students to sign up at the club, or in one case I heard you actually had to open your own club and give the proceeds to the parent club to grade. I'm sure money has no bearing on any of those grading decisions...

Worse than grading myself is having to watch one of my students take a grading. For me it's the most nerve racking and headache-inducing experiences. I take a real pride in getting the student as ready and prepared for the test as I can, and there is nothing I want more in the world than for them to achieve whatever they want to within the art. I've been known to hide my eyes when a student is out there, it's absolutely fucking excruciating. I've been lucky, only once has a student failed a grading, and they were very capable of passing they just had a bad day/weekend. That particular student had passed their second Dan exam some years before despite a broken foot that they just ignored, and a stomach they got having eaten a chilli the night before that had 40 chillies in it, so as you can imagine they had to have a pretty bad weekend to fail. They passed the next time they took the test, and I was made up for them, but also for myself. Nothing makes you happier as a teacher than watching a student progress. Well, that and being given booze at Christmas.

Iaido wisdom of the week: Grading

Yup. Pretty bloody obvious one.

Firstly, in-house gradings. At our dojo we operate the following system: there are 2 gradings to be passed at the dojo before moving to the national governing body's gradings. First is sankyu (third kyu), then nikyu (second kyu). These are to prepare you for what's ahead. Not every club does this the same way. I belonged to a club that made you go from 7th kyu to 2nd, charging good wedge along the way. I don't charge for gradings, and the flip side of that is you don't know when grading tests will be. I'll ask you to do one when you're ready. If you pass them both you're ready to try the first of the national tests. If you pass that then you are awarded Ikkyu. The next stop is Shodan (first dan).

National gradings have clock restrictions dependant on things such as time you've been a member, and when you passed your previous grading. The idea is there's a minimum study period between the grades. Also, it encourages you to maintain your membership, which you should do anyway.

So, should you grade at national level when you're ready to?

I've asked this question of various contemporaries of mine, and there's a lot of opinion about this, but ultimately it should be up to you. I was always taught that in order to show your teacher respect you should grade to demonstrate that you're listening and improving and are grateful for the teaching. That may be so, but I can see improvement every training session of my students, so is grading really necessary? Not really.

I think what is really necessary is for each individual to understand why they train, what they get from it, and whether they need gradings and milestones within that training, and therefore want the rank and responsibilities from it. I've got no problems with anyone's desire to grade and will support them to advance within it providing the syllabus and knowledge needed, and also the opportunities to do the necessary to achieve it. However, I also think that if a student has no aspirations to grade, then that's just fine too.

Just be comfortable with your choices. There is nothing to stop you changing your mind later.

Do understand though that getting ready to take a grading can be tough work. I've had students that have said they want to go up the ranks, but haven't put the hours in to do that, and haven't gotten far. It's not a piece of piss. Don't ever think it will be. Put in the work though and the rewards are there.

The best thing to do though is just keep working at your Iai and improving it and making sure you enjoy it.

You're not actually Japanese, mate

Iaido attracts a lot of people that frankly have a serious boner for Japan. Most have been there for a visit. Some go to train there for a period of time. Others have lived there for a number of years. Others have watched an awful lot of anime. Whatever the reason there are those who are borderline obsessive about Japan.

The first example of this was when I visited the Will Adams Festival in Gillingham, Kent for the first time. For those that don't know the name, William Adams was born in Gillingham in 1564. In 1600 he travelled to travel to Japan as a navigator of a ship that managed to actually reach the country (others didn't), and he is credited as the first Englishman in Japan. He is also the only Westerner to be made Samurai (There's an awful lot more to this story and I suggest reading up on it, as it is interesting).

Gillingham, although the right town to have the festival, feels a very strange place to have it. The town is twinned with Ito and Yokosuka, and has this unique story, yet the story is not taught in schools to my knowledge, and the reason we're twinned remains a mystery to most. For example: I passed the Will Adams monument for 25 years before even enquiring as to what it actually was.

The festival is in big park, and there's usually not very much to hold people's attention. There's a calligraphy tent, a reiki tent, and a few others, then the usual food, a stand where there are the aforementioned martial arts displays are found, and a person dressed as Will Adams being dragged around on half a boat. There are also a lot of non-Japanese there dressed in silk kimonos and attire, nothing to do with the festival, wandering around like an exhibit. They're not asked to come along and do it, they just fancy being seen out.

Since then, I've met lots of people in the art that try to learn the language, with varying amounts of success. Some are fluent, but far funnier are those that faux pas trying to use it incorrectly. I was at the festival with my friend and his then wife who happened to be Japanese. One of the students approached her and said something, to which she burst out laughing. He was trying to say 'you are very pretty'. Instead, it came out 'you are a pretty virgin'. The same friend was once at a meal talking about metal folding used in swords. He meant to say 'metal folding' in Japanese. Instead, he said 'bald balls'. You could have made an omelette with the egg on his face.

I've not been to Japan, and I'm not likely to in these covid times, but I admit there is a strange attraction. Each documentary or series I've seen about it shows it as being a different world from here, and I can understand the appeal of wanting to experience those differences, from simple things like music and food to other things like seeing the history and architecture. Martial arts are synonymous with Asian countries, but you don't need to experience them in Japan, as they're everywhere, including your local church hall. Watching them in Japan isn't better than watching them locally. To me it's like when people go to Dublin and drink Guinness, making out like it tastes better there than anywhere else. Like fuck it does, it tastes the same absolutely everywhere.

When the Japanese Sensei come to the UK they are treated like Gods. They give up their time to help train the higher graded

Sensei here in particular, as well as students in attendance, so that they can cascade the information down to everyone else, so it's reasonable behaviour to make sure they're looked after, fed and watered, and given some wedge. I've always felt it must be difficult for them being here too. Being looked after is one thing, but I would find it awkward being surrounded by sycophant students desperate to carry their bags, try speaking to them in pigeon Japanese, and offer to wipe their arses. It can be too much. I've watched students free practicing kata in front of the Sensei whilst they're trying to eat their lunch. They must be thinking 'fuck off and leave me alone for half hour, will you?'

It can be tense receiving instruction from the Japanese. You don't want to offend or piss them off, and you're already nervous as they approach you, but then you also have to worry about 'Honne and Tatemae'. Honne is what the teacher really thinks, in this case about your Iai, and tatemae is them telling you 'What you want to hear', such as you're doing well, when actually you suck. It can go to your head that the Japanese Sensei said you were succeeding and can backfire when you go to grade later on and fail miserably.

Iaido wisdom of the week: Thursday

Ohio (State University) Gozimas,

Named after the famed samurai Yakashimo Thursdai, Thursday is the official training day of Iaido dojo across the whole of the UK and every dojo opens for training then. Unless the hall has Zumba that day, in which case they do Iaido on another day, but begrudgingly.

In June, it's customary to turn up at the dojo ready to practice Shoden armed with snacks that your Sensei likes (this tradition goes back several hundred seconds). Beef jerky is a staple of this tradition. Just saying.

I like to weave in cultural education with the skills teaching.

Politics and playing with someone's ball

Every organisation has politics, people playing for power, insincere people wanting control, and sincere people that really want to make a positive contribution because they actually care.

The governing body we belong to is absolutely no different. People have lot of differing viewpoints on things, and sometimes they lose perspective and push their agenda much too far because rightly or wrongly they believe in it, or benefit from it. The bad news is that it can really sour your experience of the martial art. The good news is that it is (at least trying to be) a democracy, and you get to have your say and have your vote.

It takes a mighty pair of bollocks to stick your neck out at Annual General Meetings and say what you're thinking, risking ridicule and embarrassment, in the hope of making a good suggestion. It's a shame that for some it's so nerve racking, because there are people there that like the sound of their own voices, and a little less of those voices and some fresh ones would really help make it a better organisation.

Volunteers give up their time to make the association work and are often treated very badly for doing this. It's easy for a keyboard warrior to abuse one of these volunteers for not getting their way, and it's just not right, especially if they're giving nothing of themselves too. If you remove these volunteers, everything comes to a grinding halt. They work behind the scenes to sort out all the administration, they set up events, work out the finances, sort legal issues, sort adult and child protection, and a load of other things, and spend hours of their time doing it all for free.

I've been one of these volunteers. I had enjoyed membership for a few years, and I think it's important to contribute to an organisation if you take from it, and I had. I'd been to weekend training days, I'd been to competitions, and I'd enjoyed dojo life.

Maybe I'm fuck stupid, but I assumed that martial artists would be a bit more zen like, but nothing breaks a student's zen as much as you not replying instantly to their emails, or Facebook messages, or sometimes ridiculous demands.

On the day I was elected, I was proud as punch. It was in the AGM, with about 100 people there. I had a round of applause (and that hasn't happened since I dropped plates at my part time job as a waiter), I stood up so everyone knew who I was, and sat back down nervously, ready to take on my responsibilities. A short while later it was time for my training. We sat down and spent 12 hours straight going through all the systems and all the processes as I furiously made notes about it all, trying to remember what to do. Then came a piece of advice just before I left, a piece of advice that was going to keep me in good stead for the next few years. He told me that I would need to make fair decisions and stick to them, and that I would need to be thick skinned because people were going to be pretty nasty. I thought he was probably exaggerating at the time.

One of my jobs was to look after the programme that was the membership web portal. Password resetting, decisions on fees, and a number of other things came under my remit. It was created and implemented by another member some time before, and frankly for an organisation of our size it was a brilliant piece of code. You could log in online, renew your memberships, buy tickets, check student's details, and do all sorts of things, which removed most of the paperwork and cheque handling of years before. It was really great, so it always baffled me when people would email me telling me what a pile of shite it was when the issue was obviously user error. One time a guy sent me an email telling me it a disgrace that we use a piss poor system like that, and wouldn't it be better if we used a system similar to HSBCs? I replied back to them checking with them that their viewpoint really was that our little association of 2000 odd members should stump up the cash to get a system like multi billion pound bank HSBC? They replied simply saying, 'You know what, it's not such a bad programme after all'.

I can honestly say that when people want to be shit, they can be really shit. People might email with a problem, which would often be vague in terms of details and information, then if I hadn't emailed the following day fixing it, they would simply go ballistic at me. I spent more time asking people for membership details and a breakdown of the issue than achieving anything positive. There was a disturbing amount of self-important people too. Someone would miss that they had made a payment, and then I would ask them for the missing money, and then I'd get an email with such irrelevant bullshit as 'In all my 25 years in martial arts as an Aikido student as a 6th Dan etc etc'. What the fuck has that got to do with anything? I couldn't care less if you're fucking Bruce fucking Lee, you pay your fees unless you have a good reason. The fact that you've had a hobby for a long time don't impress me much.

Honestly though, this was just the tip of iceberg. I worked it out that my 'few hours here and there' voluntary job, on a regular week, took up about 6 hours. In busy periods it was that during the week and 12 to 15 hours of your weekend. It was pretty full on.

I was sitting next to a dojo colleague many years ago. There was some bickering going on between an older student, and a younger one. The younger member had suggested a change to the way something was done; quite a logical and sensible suggestion, and the older member absolutely blasted them because that's not the way the association 'do things'. The colleague leaned over to me and quietly said, "They're quite happy for you to play with the ball, just as long as you know it's 'their ball'". He was right. People think that because they've been a part of it and contributed for it for a very long time that it's theirs.

The fights for power seem to happen each year, and there are divisions and arguments aplenty. The funny thing about a martial art is that the higher grades are often revered and admired, so you think they're going to be quiet and thoughtful during these events, and when they speak you think it's going to be insightful and inspiring. What I have found though is that some of them come out of these events badly, often really very badly, with some of the most obnoxious and ill-informed comments of the whole event. They seem to happily abuse other teachers of their rank which I find really distasteful, and often really don't hold back. If martial arts give you humility and wisdom it doesn't always show, and it clearly doesn't teach diplomacy.

I learned a lot from this experience. You need to be involved behind the scenes to really see how much goes into it. So many people spend a lot of their time working hard so that others have a simple and enjoyable experience. Take arranging a weekend of training in a venue somewhere. Someone has been to the venue, checked it over as suitable and gone through the pricing structure. They've then brought that information back to the officer in charge of the art. They've then checked the calendar and contacted another officer who will post on the website and email the students to say when it is, then on the system they'll produce tickets to buy. The Treasurer will then work out how many tickets are needed to cover the costs and what the costs are. Another officer will start to contact and arrange teachers, and then work out things such as accommodation, how to feed them, how it's going to work. Someone works out transportation for those that need it. On the day, someone is there checking students in and making sure they're on the list, and then there's all the teachers required to be there to make grading students legit. It goes on and on. This is just scratching the surface of what's needed. This is one event, over 2 days.

Iaido words of wisdom: Kotsu

Refers to progression. Or, more specifically the ancient Japanese concept of not thinking you can run before you walk, because you'll fall on your tits. No one likes sore tits.

It's good to learn all the sets of your style (in Muso Shinden Ryu for example, Shoden is the entry level set, Chuden is an intermediate set, and Okuden are the advanced sets), even if you're a relative beginner. It gives you a taste of what's to come and gives you kata to wheel out at embu time when you're feeling a little fruity, but the truth is that you can't do Okuden justice until you've grasped Chuden, and Chuden will really suffer until you've done a lot of Shoden practice. This is why your grounding in Seitei is so important. Seitei is the DIY store of the Iai world, it's where the tools are. Seitei is the foundation in which your Iai will grow. Like manure on crops.

So, as we learn Seitei, we will be giving various areas of Koryu and damn good stab (see what I did there?) and the hope is that it will give you some insight into the tools you'll need to go forward, and the bits you'll want to work on. I said 'bits'. Mmmm.

I'm going back to my sandwich now.

The competitive edge

There are not many opportunities for competitive Iaido in the UK. There's a main National contest held once a year on what always seems to be the hottest and least comfortable day of the year, and there's a smattering of other competitions, often arranged by a dojo with invites given out.

My first National Championship was quite an experience for me. I was picked up in the morning by another student, a guy who I'd instantly taken a liking too when I'd joined the club, in a ridiculous sports car like that looked somewhat like KITT, and he drove it across town like a fucking idiot to collect another student before we set off for the sports hall.

When we arrived, there were a number of students milling about, and we bimbled over and chatted to them whilst we waited to go in and get changed. I found a photo recently that was taken outside as we waited and looking at the picture it saddens me that I'm the only person in it that still practices Iaido.

Several farts and knob stories later we wandered in and got changed and headed into the main hall.

I'd only been training 8 or so months at the dojo, and at the club at any one time there were roughly 10 or 12 people in a session. Here in the hall, there were what seemed like hundreds of students, dressed up, and stretching away. It's an intimidating sight the first time. Everyone looks at you. Everyone looks younger and thinner. You find a corner and put your bag down, oil up your sword and look longingly at your packed lunch, then make your way to the court where you'll be competing. It's always chaos as everyone signs in and is allocated a group.

On this occasion we all got a bollocking from a senior student for speaking loudly. No one actually tells you that you're meant to be quiet. No one actually tells you anything, to be honest. I've been lucky enough to avoid further bollockings from that person, but I have witnessed them chewing out the Mudan (beginners) on a number of occasions. It's like a rite of passage. Once it's happened, you're one of the guys. I'd high five the new guys but I'd just get a bollocking too.

The competition in the morning is divided up so that each grade has an individual competition: there's a first Dan competition, a second Dan competition, etc, and a Mudan or ungraded competition. The format is simple, you're put in a pool against 3 others, and if you win enough, you get through to the elimination stage, and then when there's one left you essentially have the winner. The winner gets a trophy made of plastic that falls apart very easily.

The rokkudan, or 6th Dan student's competition is always held first so that they can officiate the other grades rounds straight after along with the 7th Dans who don't compete (although they occasionally do a display if there's time). The 6th Dan competition is my favourite part of the whole day and is for me far too brief. You get to see some of the best at the martial art in the country doing their kata competitively, which always raises their game, and the standard goes through the roof. 8 months into Iaido and I had already become aware of how difficult some of it is, and how hard going on the body it is, and here you are watching people make it look like child's play. There was more to be impressed by though than the kata alone. After each round I became very aware of the attitudes of some of the contestants after they had won or lost. The people that lost seemed really happy (and not fake happy) that their opponent had won. There was no animosity, and if there was ego, they certainly didn't show it. I have won a few bouts and lost a few bouts over the years when I've attended, but my reaction to both is always the same because of what I saw on the first day by those people. I've never gloated, and I've never gotten annoyed, I just walk off like I've done it before and it's not a big deal. Of course, you do care, and you might be screaming inside, but it's really good to be respectful. Anyway, there's always more training to be done, regardless of the result.

The Mudan section was much larger than all the other competitions. The 3 kata we would be doing were announced and sadly my standard at the time meant that one of the forms chosen did not play to my strengths, but the other two I was quite comfortable with. I watched the other competitors that went first, blissfully unaware of whether my standard would be better or worse, and just hoped that when I went out there, I didn't make a total prat of myself. As usual.

Something happened that hadn't occurred to me might happen. My name was called, but also my dojo mate who had driven me there's name was called as my opponent. He had been practicing for a few years at this point, so when I walked out onto the floor, and I remember thinking that if I'm going to lose then it's no shame to lose to someone more experienced. There was always the chance of this happening as I was greener than the hulk's bell-end.

It's pretty frightening the first time you go out. I don't like being front and centre of anything particularly, and when you realise that there's a good-sized portion of the room watching (and it's early in the day so nobody is bored and switched off yet) as well as three judges it can make your titties tingle a bit. The word Hajime was shouted which meant it was time to start. My knob was beginning to retract at this point.

I remember being particularly pleased with myself after the first kata. The funny thing is it was probably total crap, but I was too new to know the difference, but ignorance is bliss. The second went okay but I remember nerves getting to me a little and as I put my sword away, I could hear it rattle a bit as my hand shook, and I remember very little about the last kata other than I pulled myself together a bit, and I didn't face plant, or fart loudly.

I stepped back to the line and waited for the result. The flags were raised, and they all went my way. I had won, and this raised a number of questions. What had happened to my opponent? Had he ballsed it up? And worse still, what if I make it through the group and into the sudden death, will he hang around or would I need to find myself a lift? The way back was probably not going to be as chatty as on the way there.

I managed to limp through to the quarter finals where I was eliminated by a guy who was frankly really good, and also still is really good. No shame in that.

I'd learned a lot from the day. One of the real eye openers was watching some of the other contests with people more experienced than me, but still fairly low-graded students. Some were really very impressive, and it gave me something to aim at in terms of what I would like me Iai to be in a few years. There were not all positives to take away though, some were getting really aggro when they lost. One turned around after the flags were raised, stomped off and mouth 'oh fuck off'. It just reinforced what I'd seen before though. At these events try and behave like a 6th Dan. It's more dignified than behaving like a scolded child.

The drive home was okay. He'd lost all of this fights and put it down to just having a bad day. My day was steadily getting worse though as the faster he drove on the motorway the more chance there was of instant death in an accident.

Being a competitor is a very different experience to watching your students compete. I never push any of my students to do it, it's entirely up to them, but I definitely think it's a worthwhile experience, even for a real beginner. It's a chance for them to go along and see what's ahead if you continue to practice. Yeah, you can watch Iai on YouTube, but seeing the matches and feeling the tension and stress is a better example. You don't see the sweat. As the teacher, you just really want your students to put up a good fight, and to gain from the experience, win or lose. One of my guys entered the Mudan competition one year. He'd been practicing for a couple of months and even though he knew the chances of winning any matches were almost non-existent he still wanted to give it a go. I fucking love that attitude. On the day people probably didn't notice him as he wasn't a finalist or a highly graded competitor with skills upon skills, but he made every match difficult for his opponents, even winning the odd match, and I was the proudest person in that room day.

Not all competition losses are the student's fault, or even a bad thing. I'd not long been dating my now-wife when she entered the tournament. It was my fault she lost that day, as she was very tired…

Iaido wisdom of the week is: Shu ha ri.

This is one that turns up in grading written exams quite often. It's a concept that is used to describe a student's progression (kotsu) through training.

'Shu' means conservative. It's learning fundamentals and kata. Where you are stepping, where you are cutting, who you are looking at, why you're moving that way.

'Ha' means break, which more specifically relates to a breakthrough in your understanding and going beyond the mechanics of just doing a kata or form. Increased flow, smoother movement, correct cutting, more nuanced Iaido generally.

'Ri' is the most advanced form of learning. When I fully understand it, I'll write more about it. Sometime around 2082, around my 106th birthday, give or take.

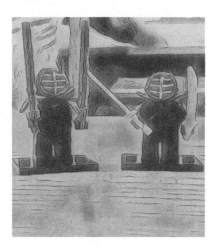

The mystique of the martial art teacher

There was an advert years ago that attempted to persuade people to train to be a teacher (primary schools were struggling) with a slogan that was something about 'never forgetting a good teacher'. This is certainly true for me, as nearly 30 years after I left school, I can still name the best ones I had, and when I remember them it's true to say the effect they have had on my life has been very significant. The sad thing is though that if you asked someone to name the shit teachers, they had they can probably reel off even more names and back them up with terrible stories about their dodgy experiences with them.

Martial arts are no different. If you've tried out a few of them over the years, you'll no doubt have experienced a number of teachers and have stories of your own to tell.

My first Judo teacher was brick shithouse of a man. Short, wide, and solid as they come. He had total command of us annoying and smelly kids, and you did not dare make a noise when he was talking. He had a way of shutting you up with a look. He ran various classes over a week, and some nights the students were a little older and you could get quite a lot achieved in a session. He really seemed to enjoy kids getting better, and if you had any aptitude for learning he would really push you to improve. I used to go home absolutely buzzing after a class. I'd go home and throw my brother (who didn't learn judo) around and try out all the moves I'd been shown, which he really didn't appreciate. What's the point of having a brother if you can't arm lock them from time to time in a hold-down that they didn't expect?

My children took up Judo a few years ago and it was a real experience to go back down memory lane and watch the classes. Their teacher was absolutely brilliant. He clearly loved what he was doing, and the kids all were potty for him. He had the same role-model qualities that my teacher had. How do they put up with parents of the kids though? Holy shit. I won't teach kids, I don't think Iaido the right hobby for them, but it isn't just that, I couldn't deal with the parent hassle.

Judo parents are bloody awful. At competitions they scream at their kids, most who don't appear to be completely happy that they are there, until they go horse. I've seen some practically go onto the mat to shout at other people's kids. I once watched a parent grab the judge of a match between two 5-year-olds at a tournament and try and argue the decision as their kid had lost (seemed pretty obvious that the kid had lost, he'd spent more time on his back than standing up). Judo is advertised as a discipline that teaches so many positive things, yet there's a load of parents there undoing them. Is it really a healthy thing to let your kid see you yelling at the referee? What sort of lesson are they going to learn there?

The first Kendo teacher, who I briefly referred to earlier, seemed a troubled man who, despite talking endlessly about himself, I really know very little about personally. I have been to other Kendo clubs since then and the format he used to teach class was pretty similar, so that seemed legit in retrospect, but his style of teaching was very much for you to just have a go and try and keep up. Kendo is a complicated martial art for a beginner to get their head around, and I would ask questions I thought were pertinent, and often wouldn't get an answer. This I struggled with. Maybe I asked shit questions and he didn't feel like answering them, I don't know. I remember asking what the yellow piece of wire along the shinai was for (I know now it represents the back of the sword), but he didn't answer. The result was I cut with it facing the opponent instead of having the shinai the other way round. Everyone is different and maybe there are a lot of students that thrive from this way of receiving information, but I just couldn't learn from it with any consistency. The other problem was that he never made me feel welcome. Again, this could be my fault. Maybe it was just a personality clash, maybe I was a bad student, and maybe he was a bad teacher. It didn't work out. The way it all turned out for me I'm pleased because had it have all clicked, I likely would never have walked into my first Iaido class.

My first Iaido teacher is in many ways my Iaido idol (say that after a few glasses of dark rum). If I could have my Iaido look like his, I'd be made up. If I could be more like him, well, that would be pretty good too. Funny thing is my Iai would never look like his. I'm over 6 foot and he's probably not even 5 foot tall, so it's not like we'd look similar at all, unless he was up close and I was really far away from you, maybe. I don't remember having a teacher of any subject with more patience than that man. He knew to pick on only one aspect of your training at a time and to try and correct that, and not to try and fix the whole broken package. That way each session you made a little improvement and as long as you practiced hard you got to retain it and get better and better. He never got frustrated if you weren't improving either, he would just keep chipping away at you. The other thing was that he was very honest with you. He would still tell you if you were getting things right, but he never felt the need to lay the boot in (and he could, there must have been some pretty ropey martial arts shown to him in my years there). Always encouraging, always positive. I try to pass that element to my students.

When you go to a national training day you get a chance to be taught by a variety of teachers and all are well respected and very competent. Whenever I was allocated to a teacher to be trained I and got allocated to him, I was always secretly really chuffed. Yes, you get to hear different angles and emphasises from other teachers, and all that will help you no end, but with him you knew you were in the safest hands there. Over the years I've had some great training sessions from other teachers where at the end of it I've walked away with a renewed enthusiasm for the art, and it's a great feeling when you know you've been worked really hard, but whenever I'd go back to the dojo I'd be taught by the most enthusiastic person for the art ever, and I would just thrive on that.

When you are part of a dojo you get to spend a fair amount of time in transport cafés, cars, pubs and restaurants with the other members. This is an added bonus to the club experience that I've always really enjoyed. We used to go on a Sunday morning to a greasy spoon café, and as we'd walk in the lady at the counter, who was fucking miserable at the best of times, would suddenly light up with she saw a particular student. She'd reach to her shoulder and fix her bra, check her hair, and as soon as he got to the counter she became a completely different person, flirting ridiculously. Then I'd get to the counter, and she'd flick the switch and revert to her usual grimacing self, look me in the eye like I'd woken her from a happy sleep, and say, 'yeah'? In the most fed-up voice.

I was in a restaurant one night after a long day of training. We noticed that one of the guys had actually slumped back and fallen asleep at the chair. We managed to decorate him and take pictures before eating his dinner, and then even had time to remove the decorations. When he woke, he continued on as if he'd eaten the meal and didn't say a word, it's like he was so shagged out he couldn't remember if he'd eaten it or not. It got him back for putting my knife and fork down his trousers when I'd be to the loo at another dinner. I had a digital camera at the time, and I'd left it on the table. The next day when I was going through the pictures, I discovered a montage of a guy putting my cutlery, which I'd used after, somewhere I did not like. I did get him back at a later date. I wasn't going to let that go unanswered.

On these trips we'd usually take turns in buying the teacher's breakfast, which he was always unnecessarily grateful for. He didn't even need to say thank you. Iaido teachers generally don't take any kind of wage for their teaching, in fact there are pretty much no perks at all. Most dojo probably don't even break even with the teachers fronting the outstanding hall fees and registration fees, so buying a breakfast here and there is a gesture that hardly goes anywhere towards the debt of teaching you. I'd try and do other things like I'd make sure I'd offer to pay fuel if he was driving, and I'd offer to do the driving as much as possible. It's nothing to do with Iaido, it's to do with good manners. This person spent 4 plus hours a week teaching me my hobby, so £20 towards fuel and a bit of egg and bacon wasn't really much of a thank you.

I don't rate myself as a teacher. I've been around so many others and witnessed their qualities that I'm very aware of things I lack. I'm quite patient, but not patient enough. I'm capable, but not as capable as those with much greater experience, and practice. I get tired and sometimes my enthusiasm wains. I can get frustrated when a student doesn't take on board what I'm trying to tell them, and don't realise at the time that my articulating of the information is the problem, and not them. What is important though is that I'm aware of these things and try and do better. You can only improve when you know what needs improving, and I really want to get better at this.

I do believe that you don't have to have the most knowledge of a subject to be the best teacher. I had a teacher at school that was an amazing mathematician and was clearly very knowledgeable about the subject. He couldn't teach it for toffee, didn't care about the students, didn't care if we kept up, and didn't want to help if we got behind. He wasn't interested.

Iaido wisdom of the week:

Mokuso

Refers to brief meditation at the start or end of the lesson.

At the start and end of the lesson I sometimes (not always) add a period of Mokuso. I do this for two reasons. Firstly, in case it comes up at another dojo or seminar (it's a common practice) you won't be sitting there wondering what's going on and you'll know what to do, and secondly to actually try to benefit from a few moments of trying it.

We do the version witheyes closed, long breaths, relaxed neck and shoulders and not the version witheyes open, mouth open collecting flies, thumbs up).

I've always been told it's to clear your mind of the daily thoughts before training, and that's how I've always used the time, and it helps with the pain of sitting in Seiza if you have that. Reading up on it it's much more involved of course, with the practitioner needing to strike a balance in their thoughts of the here and now, and an awareness of their surroundings, verses their thoughts. Whatever you choose to think about during Mokuso is of course up to you, you dirty buggers, but over time (and if you're comfortable enough in Seiza to think of anything other than pain) please experiment with it and find what works for you.

The price of training

Whenever you start a hobby it's always a concern as to what the initial costs are, and how much it'll continue to cost. Iaido is no different, and it's not necessarily a cheap hobby to have.

When you start, you might get to borrow a set of knee pads and a bokken (wooden practice sword). Dojo often offer a free session to begin with so you can get a taster, so week one can be relatively cheap. Then the costs start to mount.

Our students must join the governing body to have insurance. They have a system where you pay a tenner which gives you 3 months cover to give the martial art a real try out. Then lessons begin to need to be paid for. They vary, but a 2-hour lesson costs between £10 and £20 depending on where you practice. This is quite reasonable. I looked up yoga classes locally and they were all about £20 a session, and that was usually 60 to 90 minutes. If I joined the local archery class, it's more than that. Our lessons are £12 for 2 hours. £24 a week for 2 sessions, 4 hours total. We also do a £42 a month deal that means all sessions are available, saving some money. After the 3 months trial is up with the governing body it's up to the student if they wish to continue. If they do it'll cost the student another £25 odd quid to get the remaining 9 months of membership and insurance.

The cost of clothing in Iaido varies. You can get a set with a gi, juban, hakama and obi, all made of tetron, which is like the Ford Focus of Iai clothing, for about £100. You can purchase the same but made of much sexier material for varying amounts more, with the most expensive hand stitched Ferrari versions costing around £500. A single set will last you years though. I recently gave a new student a set that was 15 years old, and still in good condition. He seemed very grateful, even though he had my name written on his arse in Japanese.

Knee pads are something that I find really perplexing in regard to Iai. You need to protect your knees as there is an awful lot of kneeling down and getting up in the art, and over the years I've tried so many different varieties of pads trying to find a brand I really like. Martial art stores sell knee pads, but in my experience, they are either so thick that when you kneel in them the tops of your feet have extra pressure on them, or the pad is okay but the wrap slips and moves so the pad hardly stays in place. My usual go to has been volleyball knee pads. They're less thick, and the wrapping holds them in place pretty well, but they don't last very long before the padding has become a perfect mould of my kneecaps and the protection isn't as good. They're about £16 a set, so I tend to budget a few pairs a year. Other options are available; I've known people use all sorts. One of my teachers cut up his daughter's old wet suit and used strips of that, and they lasted ages. Another Iai colleague of mine uses industrial plastic knee pads, which offer great protection. The downside is you can hear them bashing on the floor each time he kneels. Some don't wear knee pads at all, and it's something I've tried and regretted 20 minutes into a session. Nothing distracts you more than the pain of your knees when dragging them across a floor.

A bokken is the weapon you usually start to train with before moving onto a metal sword and is sometimes required for training on future occasions. You can get them online and delivered for around £30-£40, and they come in various woods. You can spend more and get a plastic saya (scabbard) which gives you the full getting ready for a real sword' experience, but the saya isn't necessary as you can get around it.

Then there's the sword. When do you buy one? My policy is when I say the student is ready for one and they've demonstrated a level of competence that they could handle getting it out and putting it away without plucking out an eye, but other dojo have different rules on this. I tend to try and get the student to hold off until near the end of the three-month trial period so that they're really sure they want to continue practice without blowing a load of wedge on something that will collect dust if not used. Some are ready quicker than others, and some, especially the fantasists, get really frustrated when by week two I haven't said for them to buy a sword yet. They'll just have to pose with some other shit whilst they wait.

Swords are not cheap. If you're tall they're even less cheap. The good news though is that once you've bought it, if you look after it and treat it with respect, it will last a lifetime. An iaito, an alloy sword with a sharp point but a blunted edge, will start at around £300, and that's for a properly basic one, then the costs for something better will rocket upwards. I also want to stress something about the term blunted. The sword is not razor sharp, but 'not razor sharp' does not particularly mean blunt. You can ram it into your hand very nicely (I know) and whilst your hand won't fall off after this (razor sharp swords can cause your hand to do that) it can really damage you if you're not sensible. And don't even consider having salt and vinegar crisps after you've done it.

What makes a good sword? Depends on what you want. Some opt for something blingy (you can get a lot of fixtures and fittings to visually change your sword. I'd say improve but that's not always the case, some show you their lovely new sword, but it looks a bag of bollocks), but the really important things are that it's the right length for you, the right weight for you, and the right balance. Unfortunately to get those things costs money.

So, how's the costs all racking up for year one? Here are some very approximate ballpark figures based on what we charge and how much things cost:

A year of training at £50 a month	:	£600
Bokken and knee pads:		£56
Gi, Juban, Hakama, Obi		£100
Membership to governing body		£35
Sword (approx. for an Iaito)		£350
Total for year one:		£1141

The good news is that the years that follow don't include the bokken or the sword, or the threads, and the membership also drops a bit, so you're in the ballpark of £825.

The bad news is though that there's even more to spend money on. The weekend training days aren't included in this. If you wanted to attend a 2-day seminar it'll put you back around £50 or £60 quid. Add in travel and accommodation on top, and it's an expensive weekend for some (God help you if you pull, then it'll be even more expensive). Then there's grading. If you've trained hard and reached the chance of the next grade then the test will put you back around £25, and if you pass there's a fee for the certificate, which goes up in price as you grade (you receive the same piece of card for passing though, it just has the new grade written on it). You can't grade every year though, so there's time to save up in between.

Iaido word of the week: Kihon

Basics or fundamentals.

For those that have trained for a year or more with me will know that I think basics are very important.

I often revise how to hold the sword, go through what the parts of the sword are, and explain things like how to cut, how to perform noto, how to step, and all things fundamental to any kata. It's easy in Iaido to want to learn the most complicated kata and crave interesting difficult techniques, but without solid fundamentals there's just no point (except on the end of the sword).

Every session I spend a minimum of 30 minutes working you on these aspects of Iaido, and generally I choose Kihon that will be used later in the kata I'll be teaching. It helps set the tone of what I want to achieve in the lesson, and it knackers the students out a bit, so they won't talk back to me as much.

I do have favourites and you'll know them all by now, but sometimes it's nice to visit another dojo and see what they do as they'll probably be different things they've dreamed up. Also, I find Kihon gets you in the mood. For Iaido, not sex, obviously. If it does get you in the mood for sex, then hakama porn may be your thing.

The wall of certain uncertainness

When you first start a hobby like Iaido, every lesson is satisfying. Every time you are taught something new, whether it be how to tie your belt up, or your hakama, or a new kata, or a concept, or how to move in a certain way, and it feels good. You are learning and retaining information, and each lesson you improve rapidly from where you were the previous lesson. In a few short weeks you go from not knowing anything at all, to being able to keep up with the other students to a greater or lesser extent.

I loved this feeling when I first started. I found it motivated me and made me want to learn more and get better. It became an addiction; I didn't want to miss a single moment of the session, let alone miss a session. I wanted all the gear ASAP, and I wanted to get better and be respected.

Then, about 6 months in I hit a wall. I was trying to practice a particular technique, and I wasn't doing it well at all. The teachers were trying to help me, but the advice just didn't seem to sink in. It wasn't like I wasn't trying or didn't care; I was completely invested in trying to get it right and follow the instructions, but it wouldn't click. No problem, I thought, I'll just get it right next time.

Next time came and the problem was the same. Different teacher this time, same information, lots of encouragement still, but the same result. I just couldn't do it the way they were telling me. I continued to try but no matter what I did the result was the same. The teachers didn't seem at all concerned, but I was.

I started to wonder what was wrong with me. Why couldn't I do this relatively simple thing? It didn't look particularly complicated.

What I was being told made sense. Out of desperation I had a look in a book about it and the same information was all there. I was bloody annoyed. Was I really so shit that I couldn't do this simple thing?

Another few sessions of this and I was beginning to think that I should give up. I got changed after practice one day and slumped off into the car park, chucking my gear in the boot and feeling pretty dejected, considering changing my hobby to something less complicated. A student that I got on well with walked past towards his car and asked me if I was okay (maybe he heard Radiohead playing in my car and was concerned)? I said no I wasn't, and I explained what was pissing me off so much. "Ah, that's the wall" he explained. So, I asked him what he meant by that?

He explained that with his development periodically he would have instances where suddenly he couldn't seem to elevate his training and he felt like he'd come to a stand-still. In essence he felt like he wasn't improving. In reality though, he was improving, it was just that all the cheap and easy to take on board things weren't as readily available as once they were, so improvements are more subtle and less frequent. He explained that you become more aware that you're not doing it right. When you first started you didn't know anything and were happy with everything you did. Now you know more about what you need to achieve, and it's not that you aren't continuing to learn, it's that you appreciate what you have to do and that it is going to be harder work from now on. His advice was to keep working, keep trying, and eventually I'd get it. So that's what I did. I kept trying. A few weeks later I performed the technique and the teacher nodded and said, 'that was nice, keep it up'. Hearing that was like hearing that the hottest girl in school was going to be your date for the prom, that she'd booked the hotel and she'd bring the beer too. And a friend.

I've hit the wall many times over the years. What I have noticed is that the satisfaction from moving past these walls is every bit as good a feeling as when I first started training. It happens much less often, but when it does, I get a high like nothing else. These days when these walls happen, they take longer and longer to get past, but when you work it out and make the changes it's just the greatest.

One of the more interesting discoveries I made with Iaido is: the more you learn, the more you realise you don't know. It's a strange paradox to get your head around, but for me it's the challenge of trying to constantly get better and improve when you know that each time you make a positive change that a whole new area of improvement you need to attack will open up for you, usually with something more difficult than what you just dealt with to try and change. Of all the hobbies and activities I've tried, I find Iaido to be the only one where each success comes with a realisation that you need to work harder. When you score a goal in football, it isn't twice as hard to score the next one. In Iaido you pass a grading and same day you're thinking about how many years it'll take you to pass the next one, and how daunting that will be.

The other thing about Iaido is that just because you've learned something and have done it right once doesn't mean it'll stay correct. Re-visiting your mechanics and basics frequently is really important. I start each year with a lesson where I explain how to hold the sword, where your fingers go, how to take it out and put it away. The class look at me with distain when I do this lesson, like I'm teaching them to suck eggs, but it's always a surprise how many aren't doing it right and need the reminder. You can't advance if you can't do the basics right and keeping the basics right is down to just simple hard graft. At least that's what I'm told.

With hard graft comes physical demands on you. When most students start, they can't extend their legs enough to take long steps without their heel being very high off the floor. Or they can't sit in tate hiza (which is a way of sitting with all your weight on your heel/ankle) easily or at all. Kneeling down can be painful and sitting like it even more so.

Well, there's good news. When I started I couldn't do fuck all. I had a lot of pain, couldn't stretch easily and couldn't sit in tate hiza. I didn't realise that your body, if pushed enough, would adapt allowing you to do these things. It takes time and a lot of effort, but if you keep stretching your body will start to make these things possible. Don't get me wrong, there's so much more I'd like my body to be able to do that would make it all easier but compared to when I first started the progression is remarkable. The trick is to not stop, keep at it and eventually you'll notice the change. I'm always shocked when a student a few years in can do things physically that they simply couldn't do before. It's rewarding when you see it.

Iaido can be particularly difficult to learn as different teachers see emphasis and style choices differently within the techniques and kata. I was at a training day many years ago when a 6th Dan graded teacher came over to me and told me that they didn't like my cut. I was awaiting some actual information as to what was wrong with it so I could try and make the necessary adjustments, but they didn't feel the need to furnish me with any actually useful critique on this occasion, and instead they sauntered off, hands behind their back, to impart 'useful information' to someone else. Just minutes later another teacher came past of the same grade. They watched me for a few seconds and then told me that I have a very nice cut. I hadn't changed it from my usual way of doing it since I hadn't been told what was wrong.

This isn't uncommon. I've even been at training days when a technique has been taught one way, and then another teacher has come straight over and told us that it's not correct and shown it a different way, then minutes later the first teacher has quietly come over to the group I'm in and said that the other teacher was incorrect and that the way we were shown first is in fact the right way of doing it, and to ignore that way. Both were the same level, both from the same style of lai. It's really difficult for a student to know what to do. You don't want to offend anyone. It's not like you can ask which is right. Ask them both together which is the correct technique, and both would be very respectful of each other's opinion and at the end of the conversation you'd probably be none the wiser. I've done this before, and it didn't work at all. Showing them both respect is important so I didn't question further, even though I just wanted to make the point that I'd travelled over 300 miles and spent serious money on the weekend and frankly it's shit not to have the right answer, but that wouldn't go down well.

So 'not offending' is an important lesson. At the same time, you don't want to fail a grading by doing something the wrong way, and you don't want to look stupid in the process, so it can be an infuriating situation. After a weekend one of my students explained that he was confused how to do a particular part of a kata, as two teachers had done it differently. Not just explained it differently, done a part of it differently. He wanted to know what to do? So, I gave him the stock answer I was always given. Firstly, learn both ways and practice both ways. That way if in the future it's rolled out definitively then you won't have to learn the new way from scratch. Secondly, we're all human and fuck up, so try not to get too annoyed. Look at it from the point of view of the kata. Which makes the most sense? If one is more conducive to what you would do in the situation, then go with that in the main. If you're asked why, you do it that way then at least you've given it thought. That can't hurt.

Between Gary's leg, Trevor's back, and my back going mental, it's fair to say everyone gets injured or hurt in daily life, and there are times you just can't train. But what's the protocol when you can't go to a dojo and pick up a sword?

It depends on the injury I guess, but there's really two alternatives. The first is to train around the problem. I tore a muscle in my arm, so instead of a sword I used a piece of bamboo that weighed fuck all for a few months. That way I could train. Gary is getting round his leg injury using Robocop's foot (trainers with grey covers on). When injured you do what you can. There's nothing wrong with that.

But what if it's something you can't get around?

I'd been training for only four months when I had to have an operation that meant no Iaido for three months after. That's quite a long layoff having just mastered which end is the sharp bit. I didn't know what to do and was expecting to be walking back into the dojo six or seven months after I started as an absolute beginner. So, I asked my teacher what I should do?

Firstly, he said to come along and watch if I could. Now this is really important. If you can attend and watch, and not everyone can, but if you can bring a pad and make notes, unless you're all modern and shit in which case bring your fancy pants tablet thingy. Ask questions. Not all learning involves you trying it out right there and then. I learned bags from those lessons. On top of that there's something else you notice. I thought I was really terrible compared to everyone else. Watching the class, I realised that everyone made tonnes of mistakes. Actually, I wasn't nearly as shit comparatively as I thought I was. Everyone dropped the kissaki, everyone has trouble with straight feet. I suddenly felt much better.

Second, he asked to me to online and read up. Terminology, the kata names and numbers, what they translated to, and some Iaido history.

When I came back, I genuinely came back better.

Anyway, what I'm saying is injuries don't have to mean the end of training. You can continue to train if you want to. It's up to you.

The stressed body

When I started Iaido I was in my late 20s. My body wasn't in great working order back then thanks to years of playing sports and therefore years of sports injuries. I'd broken ankles, cracked ribs, broken fingers, hurt my knees and even had the odd mild (if there is such a thing) concussion.

Watching Iaido I thought that it looked so simple and non-physical that it would be easy on the body. As I wrote earlier, your body eventually gets more used to Iaido as you practice, and that comes with elements of pain and aches. You get used to it, and it's positive, but there are other injuries and issues with your body that occur.

I used to find that 90 minutes into a session, my thighs would start to shake. The endless standing and kneeling repetitions really started to make them like jelly, so much so that I even struggled to drive home at the end of the night. It frustrated the hell out of me. It would happen at inopportune times, and I'd have to sit out until the wobble went. Eventually it just went away.

I was practicing a kata for the very first time when I felt a pain in my right foot. The kata involved me sitting in a squatted position called sonkyo for the very first time, and I managed to put a hair-sized split in a metatarsal on my little toe. This meant that every time I put any pressure on the toe the bone would open a tiny bit, and I had to be peeled off the ceiling from the pain. This led to me doing six months of standing kata only, which was vexing, but turned out to be a good thing because it meant I had six months to really focus on those forms. Sometimes the lows can be turned into positive highs.

I tore a muscle in my arm a year in because my cutting technique was really bad. I overextended the forearm constantly and cut with much too much power. One day I finished a cut and it felt like a knife had been stabbed through the arm. It hurt so much I couldn't sleep for days and struggled to drive and work easily. I went to see the doctor who, without examining me, told me I'd need to just take paracetamol. I sought out a different doctor who actually looked at it and diagnosed it. Once it healed, I went to an osteopath who beat the fuck out of me for 40 squid a pop, but it was the best thing I ever did. In fact, I recommend a six-monthly shit kicker at the osteo generally when practicing Iaido. It keeps everything in the right place.

Knee pain comes with the territory. A good training session of Iaido means kneeling and standing, kneeling, and standing all evening, as well as twisting the joints in ways they don't want to be twisted Sore knees can last a few days but on occasion I get something more concerning, which is a pain much deeper in the knee that doesn't go away for weeks. I've swallowed large quantities of glucosamine over the years, and I don't have much evidence to say that it helps, but the upside is that the pain seems to bugger off on its own.

A few years back I started getting weird spasms in my left foot. It really hurt when I was kneeling and when I was putting the foot anywhere but completely flat. My foot doctor, Doctor Heel (not making this up) couldn't find anything in particular wrong with it, but we iced it all the same and kept the weight off it for a bit. It comes and goes but only rears its head when doing Iaido. This wasn't the first problem I've had with my left foot though. Since starting Iai I now have a lump on the top of my left foot that juts out. It's about an inch diameter, and when I kneel down it bruises, instantly. My other foot Doctor, Doctor P Staker (again, I'm really not making this up) said he could remove it, but it would require the bones in the foot to be removed and replaced after cleaning them off, so I thought sod that as I doubt that would come without other issues, and I've learned to live with the pain. The first kneel down of the day hurts, then after that the pain is much less acute.

I was at Doctor Staker's when he was kind enough to ultrasound a lump on the back of my leg which had really concerned me. Turns out a muscle had moved in my leg, and it now resided much more closely to my foot. It shit me up for a while though wondering what it was.

The only other injury type I've had really is the odd accident with a sword. I haven't had one for years now, but in the early days I would poke myself from time to time. The worse one was at a training day before a grading, when a teacher came over to correct something I was doing incorrectly. In attempting to add in the detail of what I was shown I managed to stick myself in the puffy bit of my left hand between the thumb and finger. There wasn't a huge amount of claret, but the wound stung like crazy, and was distracting throughout the grading as sweat was like someone pouring salt on it. It didn't heal up for ages, so I must have gotten myself pretty well. I have seen other injuries with swords. The common injury from a blunted sword seems to happen when you go to put it away and sort of miss the entry point of the scabbard and plunge it into your hand. Fortunately, the damage is always fairly superficial, and the damage to pride seems to be the bigger issue. When you're using a shinken, or razor-sharp sword, even the smallest issues are potentially more dangerous and what would be an 'ouch' moment with a blunted

Iaito is a life-changing event with one of those bastards. I've only first-hand witnessed people cut themselves a few times, and each time people have gotten lucky. I am aware of stories of others who needed stitches and more care afterwards though. Even the most experienced practitioners fuck up occasionally. Even monkeys fall out of trees.

So, whilst Iaido lacks the physical contact of a collision sport it doesn't mean you're going to remain injury free and healthy. Iaido does have benefits too. I'm definitely more flexible now. I have better posture and in general my back feels better now than before I started. I have more physical strength than I used to have in my arms and legs too. If I concentrate on seated kata for a few months, I really notice the difference in my legs. Iaido can be a good way of building your leg strength up gradually.

Iaido wisdom of the week: Chinugui

Means 'wiping of the blood'. This is an alternative action to a Chuburi, where you shake or flick the blood off, here you place the sword ready to wipe the blood away.

This is done in various kata: Seitei number 3 ukenagashi is the one you'll see the most, but Gyakuto, Junto and Ryuto from Shoden all feature it.

They would use a Tenugui to perform this wiping action as it was the darkest part of Japan's history and Lemon Pledge was not readily available.

Taking on students from other martial arts

Some of the students have backgrounds in other Japanese martial arts. In my dojo currently we have a mix of Karate veterans, experienced Aikido students, Ju Jitsu practitioners and a Judo player.

Having studied something else does definitely have some advantages. The format of the classes for example are very familiar. The etiquette, the dos and don'ts, the stretching up, followed by Kihon, followed by some teaching of a kata or technique, the free practice of a technique etc, none of that is surprising or new when you've done something else.

The familiarity of some of the language is also a benefit. You will definitely hear terms and expressions that are common to both arts, and something you already know is something less to get your head around. When I started Iaido I could already count in Japanese, knew the names of various body parts and had a grasp of a lot of the language I'd hear in the club. A little bit of comfort zone went a long way back then, and I was smug I already had some prior knowledge.

There are of course downsides to having done other martial arts. Movement is definitely one of these. Iaido involves you moving in a way that other martial arts don't appear to. The engagement of hips towards an opponent with feet straight and posture straight has seemed an alien concept to anyone who has practiced anything else. Certainly, the beginners who have never tried anything before seem to pick this up more quickly than those who have to fight years of training in something else in order to consistently take it on board. Turning on the balls of your feet, pushing from your back foot and keeping straight does seem to be a nightmare for some, and is a clear frustration to the student, especially when someone else just picks it up like it's no big deal.

The subtle differences are a big issue to fix too. Take someone who has sat in seiza (sitting on your knees) for years. Iaido has rules as to whether you can move your feet to sit down, or that you have to move a particular foot, and when you sit there's a place for your hands, a width between your knees (that doesn't look like you're sporting massive bollocks), and if you haven't done it in this way before suddenly something as simple as sitting down becomes a massive headache to get right. It seems so simple to the person teaching it: you do this, this, and this, sorted. To the student it's yet another mountain to climb. You're always fighting the muscle memory and unless you really concentrate it can elude you.

My experience of having students from other arts has been varied. I am sympathetic to these people as I see what they're fighting against. I also know that it's probably going to be a tougher challenge to me to educate them, but I do quite like the challenge, especially when they show commitment. However, I'd be lying if I said it wasn't at times bloody irritating at times, specifically when I've had a few students who have reached high levels in the other martial arts. I find that they're really difficult to teach as every time you try and show them something, all they want to do it tell you about how they do it in the alternative art, and basically make it all about that. It brings the class to a halt for everyone else who really couldn't give a fuck that a student learns something different elsewhere because it really detracts from what they are trying to achieve with their training that day. If I have to hear 'In Aiki we do it like this' one more time… I'm sure they are different in their approaches. I've never studied Aikido and I have no desire to, but the student seems surprised when I explain that it's not my job to tell them which one is more correct in a combat situation, or more effective, or anything about it. My job is to teach what's right in Iaido. Isn't that hard enough a job without having to cross compare every martial art every time I teach a kata? "We hold it like this in Aiki". Yep, who gives a shit? Not the 5 other students, that's for sure. Each who have paid their fees to train in Iaido and not to hear a philosophical debate about nothing important. It's like halfway through learning a throw in Judo saying to the teacher, 'Wouldn't it be better if we just shot them instead?'

I've been to a lot of training weekends over the years, lots of these with Japanese teachers. I've been in lessons with people that speak Japanese fluently, and what I've noticed is that everyone pronounces words in pretty much the same way. A Hajime in one class will be the same Hajime in another class. So, when a new student came to our club one day, armed with a little bit of Kenjutsu training, I was somewhat perplexed when they insisted on loudly correcting my pronunciation of various words. I wouldn't mind but these weren't complicated words. My favourite was whenever I said the word 'noto' (pronounced no-toe), which is the instruction for everyone to sheath their sword. Each time I did it he said 'not-oh', before putting his sword away. I politely explained that it's always said 'no-toe', but for the rest of the lesson he did the same fucking thing, and I mean every single time. I asked if they spoke fluent Japanese. They didn't. One of my more senior students wandered over to me and whispered, 'I think you're being very restrained today, Sensei'.

It does bring up the question; do people do that sort of shit on purpose, or are they blissfully unaware they're being really disrespectful? Maybe it's nerves? Or maybe they're just a knob end? I don't know.

.

Iaido wisdom of the week: Boshi

The boshi is the curved area just after the very tip of the blade at the sharpest point of the kissaki.

When you draw the sword, the boshi is just being exposed at the point you release the blade, and you apply tension with your fingers so that the sword fires outwards from the saya. If your sword is the correct length, you can draw it fully with your right hand, and pull your left hand and the koiguchi to your obi, and at this point apply the tension with your fingers and thumb and the sword will come out as you begin sayabiki.

Knowing the length of your sword and being confident of where the boshi is will improve your drawing of the sword dramatically. There's nothing less Iai-sexy than pulling the sword clear of the Saya, before beginning the cut towards the opponent. You cut directly from the Saya. There's no need to draw and then cut, Nukitsuke is to cut directly from the Saya.

In other words, always be aware of your length.

The martial mystique

I once sat at a dinner table with a person from another dojo who I hadn't met before. There was a group of us and somehow the shuffle had meant me sitting opposite this person for the meal. They were very into Iaido, talking about it whenever the conversation had deviated to something far more interesting. This I found a bit like going on works drinks when you try to avoid talking about whomever in sales being a right arse, but somehow the conversation always seems to go that way despite your best efforts.

Then they asked the usual questions: grade, dojo, teacher, where in the country, blah blah. Then they asked me why I learn Iaido?

This should be a really simple question to answer since I'd at this point been practicing at least a decade or so, but actually I found that it wasn't that easy to explain. Ask a person why they do other martial arts, and you might be told they want to keep fit, or they want to be able to handle themselves in a fight. These weren't accessible answers as Iaido doesn't keep you aerobically fit, and unless you're carrying a sword on your nights out it doesn't fall under the self-defence category.

Truth is, I fancied doing something different to what I felt was the norm. I didn't want to play football. I had a number of aging mates who were playing in their late 20s and 30s and they all seemed under the delusion they were in the Premiership and not playing for a pub team. I didn't fancy that. I was too old for collision sports. I was never any good at racket sports, tennis in particular. I could serve inside the white lines, as long as it was on a different court a couple of roads away. I didn't want to do the decathlon like my more corporate friends were all doing, I thought that was a cliché and couldn't really see myself doing what I always hated which was more P.E.

Martial arts seemed to fit the bill for me. Kendo was different enough a thing. People had heard of it, even though they knew shit all about it. "Ha ha, Kendo Nagasaki"… If you say so, knob-head. This led to Iaido.

The person then piped up with their reason: "I always wanted to learn the sword. I want my body and the spirit of my sword to be as one with my mind". They person listening in to my left nodded with agreement at this statement as if it made perfect sense. My eyes were open wide at this point. What the fuck?

I have a hard time with this sort of statement in martial arts generally. It's the kind of phrase I've heard in films. But that's what they are: films. Not real, not factual, they're just entertainment. I was totally confused: I mean firstly what spirit? For me you'd have to provide evidence that there even is such a thing, unless it's meant in some other way like 'personality' or something like that, but a sword doesn't have a personality, it's just a piece of metal clipped into a wood handle which is wrapped in a material like cotton or leather (or, in my case, sometimes grime).

I get that you want to get so good at Iaido that using the weapon is completely natural and don't need to think about it at all (if that's indeed what they actually meant) but there's no mysticism about the path to get there. Ask any 8th dan how they got to that level, and I guarantee they didn't meditate in secluded forests, seek the wisdom of the elder on top of the mountain, and they didn't rub a magic lamp. They all got there because they worked hard, trained hard, listened hard, took the knocks, and bad days in their stride and kept going. And let's be honest, that menjo is just a piece of paper with their grade on it that said they passed their grading. It's a better reflection that they have a standard than any other I can think of, just shy of letting everyone come at them, swords drawn, so that they can go Tom Cruise on their arses.

There are times in training I become incredibly immersed in my training. My first Iai teacher told me once that it had only happened 3 times where he had managed to switch absolutely everything off in his mind other than Iaido, and those training sessions were the most satisfying he'd ever had. I've only had it once. I was training on a Thursday evening on my own in a poorly lit hall. I started off with the usual practice I did to warm up, and then picked one kata, and did it over and over again. Each time I did it I tried to see the opponent, and maybe it was the lighting, or because I was tired, or something else, but the combination made me exclude everything in the world outside of that reality, and for 90 minutes that's all there was. When my phone alarm went off to tell me there was 10 minutes before the Zumba class bowled in, I was thoroughly pissed off.

Did I reach an area of training of temporal grace? Did I reach a spiritual plateau? Or did I just get well into my training because there were no distractions? I'd say the latter. Others would say it was something else.

I don't know if other martial arts attract as many of this kind of 'spiritual' person as Iaido does but they probably have their fair share also. A fellow student said to me once how sad it must be to chase that dream of enlightenment through martial arts all the way through to just before death, then suddenly it comes and it's the realisation that there was nothing more to it than learning the martial art. I think that when it comes the enlightenment is this: the enjoyment and satisfaction of years of the art, the friendships and relationships that changed your life, and all the good things it brought you. Obviously, I could be wrong, but I'm too busy enjoying the ride to worry about where we're going.

Shit, did that sound poetic? Bollocks.

Iaido wisdom of the week: Seitei

This is a word you'll hear a lot.

In regard to Iaido it refers to a particular set of 12 kata.

Originally created in 1969 to make it easier for kendoka to learn Iaido, Seitei has since grown and developed to become the standardised tuition across the styles within the International Kendo Federations across the world. These are the kata that are used as the standard for promotion, and often competition outside of koryu: the traditional styles of Iaido or Batto.

The katas were created by looking at commonality between the various koryu styles of Iai, and this is evident as you learn them. The kata Ganmen Ate has roots in Yukichigi from the Okuden set of Muso Shinden Ryu for example. Similarities to Mae are evident across Koyru: Shohatto, Sato, Uto, Koranto, Inyoshintai, Yoko Gumo, Kasumi, and various others.

In practice Seitei is an excellent training tool to prepare a student for what is ahead in koryu, and it's definitely the foundation for good iaido.

Kotsu, or progression of learning, begins with Seitei. Learning to cut, learning to align your hips and engage the opponent, learning to turn your feet and move with good posture: it all begins with Seitei.
Ultimately if your seitei iai is good, you will be able to cope with learning koryu much more easily.

The coasting student

I was teaching class one day when it became apparent that a student's Iai had regressed, and it wasn't as sharp than it was maybe a year or two ago. Throughout the session I carefully watched them going through a variety of kata to see if there was a common issue: was the footwork poor and making them all look bad, or perhaps the cut wasn't right, or maybe they were just tired and dialling it in. I couldn't really identify it as a single issue. in some kata the footwork was precise, in others it all over the shop. The cut was okay, if not as sexy as you'd like it.

This particular student isn't young and often suffers from injury and physical issues, and that combined with many covid closures meant that they haven't maybe trained all that much in that time. Still the standard should be better than it seemed to be now.

I wanted to talk to them about it, but I didn't really want to come out and say that they're going backwards, and I found it a bit awkward and the last thing I would want to do is to destroy their confidence. I engaged in a bit of small talk which isn't difficult with this student as we come from fairly similar working backgrounds and that seemed to break the ice a little. I asked him how he felt his Iai was going, and he gave me his honest breakdown of his current standard (he said it was dog shit). It wasn't dog shit though, it just wasn't up to his usual standard. I expected him not to have made huge progress with all the breaks in training, but my concern was to make sure he kept the standard so that he could continue to improve on his own terms. I told him that it wasn't bad at all, and we needed to get him confident again, and that we'd work together on getting him back on track. He seemed pleased that I was going to help him move forward with his training. I said the next session we'd make a start.

I knocked up a plan of what needed working on from what I'd seen and started to make notes about his Iai and broke it down into all the different areas. Knowledge of the kata, bunkai (the situation being dealt with), basic correct footwork, posture, metsuke (use of the eyes), cuts and stabs, body movement and noto (correctly sheathing the sword).

I thought about the footwork and worked out a plan to tackle that first. I had lessons planned to have him walk through all of the kata from Seitei without a sword until they were wedged into his mind.

I thought about how to correct his cut and decided I would get him to teach the class how to cut, thus he would have to study the movement and articulate it to the other students.

I thought about his metsuke, and worked out a way where in each kata I'd have some sort of brightly coloured thing on a stick so I could get him to follow it with his eyes each time, until it had sunk in.

I thought about how to teach the bunkai of each of the kata and decided that as he walked through each of them, I'd stop him at key points and explain in detail exactly what was happening and keep doing it until he knew everyone down the finest detail.

The next session came along, and I dragged my big folder of notes in with me, ready to begin the transformation. He came in and I explained that needed to get ready quickly as we had a lot to get through.

I popped to the loo and when I came back warmups had started and this particular student was already out on the floor, going through all the Seitei kata. As I watched I noticed that all of them were really good. No particular issues with anything at all. I wandered over confused and said, 'you're looking much better today'. 'Yes', he said. 'I was just tired the other day. I'm fine now'.

On the upside I had teaching fodder for everyone for the next few weeks. I couldn't help but think, 'you bastard' though. No good deed goes unpunished, I guess.

There are times though when a student does seem to be coasting, like they're bored of Iaido and are just going to training because it's what they do each week, like it's routine. This is something that can lead to a student leaving if you don't address it. As a teacher I feel my job is to keep feeding students their next challenge to help them improve. If they don't take that challenge then that's up to them, and there's bugger all I can do about that other than encourage them to try, but if I don't work out what they need and communicate it then I'm not really doing my job. The other part to this is that you have to identify the right tasks to set them. I can honestly say that there's no formula I've found that will do this, I just have to keep observing and thinking on my feet about what they could do with changing. I get it wrong sometimes, but I do my best.

Iaido wisdom of the week: Tenouchi

Tenouchi (pronounced te-no-uchi, not ten-ouchy) means the inside of the hand.

The relevance to Iai of the term is to do with the cut, and specifically the moment the blade comes into contact with the opponent and leaves the opponent.

At the start of the cut, your grip is less tense to allow quickness of movement from the starting position to the point of impact with the opponent. Just before contact is made you increase tension in the grip with your knuckles turning out opposite very slightly to strengthen the hold and concentrate the strike, as the kissaki pulls through and heads downwards through your opponent's body. The tenser grip is seamlessly released (don't look at my cuts for God's sake) back to the more relaxed grip as the cut finishes.

A lack of tenouchi means you whip the sword at an opponent and have the chance of the blow glancing off as it's not firmly gripped, and you want to cut with precision and efficiency.

A Hachidan wasn't available

Earlier on I wrote: 'Ask any Hachidan how they got to that level, and I guarantee they didn't meditate in secluded forests, seek the wisdom of the elder on top of the mountain, and they didn't rub a magic lamp'.

I don't have access to a Hachidan as I don't speak Japanese (let alone write it), but what I do have is access to a few Nanadan, so I asked one of them how they got to the level of Nanadan in Iaido?

They wrote that these were the most important paving stones:

1. I trained regularly, not necessarily to a sweat each time, but regularly.
2. I listened to what seniors told me but I never let my brain fall out, I judged and evaluated everything I was told.
3. I was always fairly ready to throw away any idea I was carrying.
4. I kept myself in reasonable shape so I could train without injury.
5. I videoed myself frequently to avoid getting any illusions that I was good enough.
6. I paid attention to what younger, more junior people were doing, especially if they were good, and challenged myself to do it as least as well.

I know this particular Nanadan fairly well, and I've been taught by him a number of times over the years. I can say that they he easily in the company of the most committed people to the art.

He works exceedingly hard, and his Iai is one of my favourites to watch.

Like all people I like to watch I try to emulate their style as much as I can, taking the bits I like and trying to add it to my own Iai (a bit like a shit Borg). Obviously, I lack the knowledge to emulate the subtle things that lift them above others, but I've heard that the greatest compliment is imitation (and giving rum, obviously).

It's a very interesting list of criteria to me. What first jumped off the page is that they had the same neuroses and worries that I have.

Number 5 in particular is something that I really didn't expect: watching yourself, not to look at what you've accomplished but looking at yourself to see the errors you teach others not to do, and the realisation that you need to fix them. But more than that, it's a leveller, and a leveller that could drive you forward. I film my students doing Iai from time to time and keep them so that when they improve, they can look back and see it in a way that would be otherwise difficult to describe. Having read this, I plan to use it for all of my dojo to help with our next steps (literally in my case: my sticky-outty feet are my enemy in Iai).

Number 1, regular practice, is something I've believed in for years. Iaido, like many sports, rely on you reaching a level of form, and that form only maintains with regular practice. If I go on holiday for a week and then come back to training, I honestly do notice the gap. It doesn't make a huge difference to my form, but I do notice in my body that there's a little more pain when I do certain things such as kneeling. If I have a two-week gap such as Christmas time when I return it is far more significant. Worse still is recovering from illness. I had the flu (not the 'bad cold', the real flu) and when I returned I felt well enough to train, but I wasn't ready and it took weeks to get my body back, and more to get my form back. In order to improve I think you have to hit that form: the best current Iai version of you. Once you've done that you can take on extras to work on.

The 'keep in shape' comment is one myself and many others that train struggle with. My weight has gone up and down many times over the years as I have problems outside of the world of Iai and eating is my outlet. I don't smoke, I don't do drugs, I do drink but not enough to be a problem (I can go quite a long time without it), but I never saw a dinner that didn't call my name. I could exercise more, and I have had periods when I work out consistently and my fitness has been pretty good, but something happens, and I get out of rhythm with it. If you want to reach the top of any activity you have to do what's necessary, and that means in Iaido you need to be fit enough to cope with the higher levels of training, and strong enough to endure. I have no aspirations to be a high grade, it's not what drives me, so maybe I don't need to keep in shape, but I do know that if I change my mind and what to go further it's absolutely necessary.

Points 2 and 3 I've touched on already, but the idea that you need to evaluate what's being taught is absolutely critical to good Iai. You get taught different variations of the kata often, so instead of confronting the teachers as to what is right you should really think about what makes sense to the situation. Would it work? Would the timing work? Would you do something else? Are the different options purely aesthetic or would they make a real difference? But maybe the most important comment is being ready to throw an idea out completely when needed, and this is fucking hard to do when you've done it that way for years, but it surely it must be the best way of changing and improving. Keeping something that doesn't work won't benefit you at all.

The final point about the younger students is particularly frightening to me. I often watch younger, slimmer people do Iai. The ones that aren't as experienced as me often do the bits they know really well, using their younger bodies to real advantage. I watched a tall thin guy in this early twenties do a kata at a competition, and his posture was perfect, his stance was perfect, and he glided around the floor like a fucking Dalek. He had no seme, his metsuke was horrible and his angles were not great, but it didn't matter because he presented what he had so well. I came away from that competition and really tried to smooth out my movement and make stances a bit longer and straighten up my posture. That guy will be formidable in a few years' time when they combine experience and greater knowledge with their current arsenal, and yeah, I find it concerning because the one thing I can't do is make myself younger no matter how much Olay I bathe in.

Age is a great killer of confidence. I don't want to stagnate and be comfortable with myself, pottering about doing a bit of Iai and then dodging the rest of the lesson. I've been to training days and watched some students a few grades higher than me do really terrible Iai and then spend more time wandering around telling lower grades what to work on (even though they're not teaching that day) instead of actually getting off their arse and doing better Iai because it's easier, and whilst I'm grateful for the knowledge they're imparting I'm aware they're doing it so they can duck out of training. If you want to get better, you have to challenge yourself to do so and then really care about it. The Nanadan didn't mention caring about it in their response to me, but I'm pretty sure they must care about it a hell of a lot.

Iaido wisdom of the week: Kasso teki

This refers to the invisible opponent.

Iaido, as you've probably realised by now, requires you to imagine an opponent when training. Your opponent is your height, so if you're 6' 4" tall it's probably not a good idea to imagine Ronnie Corbett as your opponent.

If you're new to Iaido you're going to struggle with this for a while. It's hard enough remembering which foot goes forward or which way you're supposed to turn, but as your training progresses you will get to a point where the opponent becomes a lot more important to you.

I used to experiment with trying to imagine someone to aim at, and it did help. Trying to visualise the opponent helped me look in the right direction and made me cut straighter. It makes the whole thing feel more real and less like a dance.

What's the difference between a kirioroshi and Boris Johnson?

One's a cut...

So, Boris declared we'd have to have a lockdown in March 2020 because of some global virus thingy, and the dojo shut its doors along with most other places in the country. At first it looked very temporary, and I remember thinking that it'll be nice to have a break for a couple of weeks from training, and instead I could catch up on the important things in life like my wife and kids and Only Connect.

Three weeks in and it started to look less like it was going to be a short break and more like it was going to be a full-on hiatus with no club. Weirdly I had a lot of dojo enquires at this time asking when we'd be opening next. I always think I'm out of loop with the news, but it was interesting to see that there were hermits that wanted to try Iaido. I mean, seriously?

People around the UK started to join online training, with higher grades trying to train from their front rooms, tables pushed out the way, and students around the country trying to follow on without twatting their ceilings. It was kind of a beautiful time to be part of something where people would go the extra mile in just trying to do some of their hobbies, and everyone doing their bit to keep it going. One of the high grades even started teaching Japanese for free to anyone that wanted to do the video lessons. It was a unique time to be alive with a solidarity that lacked when everything was open and no one had heard of Corona virus,

Covid 19, and thought Lockdown was a group from the 90's that did the track Gunman.

We started training in the garden which I think confused the neighbours who could hear the odd swoosh of the sword and would scurry upstairs to twitch their curtains. The weather was pretty good, and we (me and her) managed to get outside a fair bit. Teaching is really weird when you're in the open and neighbours can hear what you're saying, so I got really self-conscious and gave much less information than I normally would, and instead went with the nod or the suck air through teeth approach. Just before the lockdown we had got the garden sorted and had artificial grass laid which is not a bad surface train on. Gets bloody hot in the summer though, but no sign of grass on your knees.

While it was no substitute for the real thing. It kept our hand in and it kept us interested for a while at least, but putting your clobber on and tooling up to stand in the garden is not the same experience as a dojo: The welcoming of students, the smell of the hall, the sound of laughter, the noise of brooms moving the glitter and dust around, the smell of clove oil on your sword, and the sound of cracking limbs as everyone kneels, it's something that bird song and barbeque charcoal cannot be a substitute for.

Eventually Boris lifted the lockdown, the dojo re-opened and most of the students rocked up, heavier, less fit, but more motivated than before to get into it. We lost a couple of students, both not willing to take the risks of walking back into areas occupied by people, and potentially a virus that could really harm or kill them. I respect for that decision; everyone must make their own choices in these times and if they weren't comfortable then it would be wrong of me to object, and I wished them well.

It wasn't too long before we were cracking on like nothing had ever happened. One of the students whose training was always buggered up from shift work was furloughed and could come to every session, and their level rocketed up from the consistent attendance. It felt like a privilege to be able to do this. Many other sports and arts were still taboo, restricted because of the inability to distance whilst training. My daughter's Judo class not being able to open any time soon, my wife's Yoga class restricted attendance because of the need for social distancing, but Iaido is the 'social distancing' martial art because you have to stay two sword lengths' apart. I was grateful because otherwie I still have been at home playing Swordsman VR on the PS4 and putting on even more blubber instead of actually training.

Come October the numbers of covid deaths were rising in the UK and it looked like we were destined to be closed again. There was a growing tension in the dojo, like we all knew that next time the lockdown was going to go on longer, and the uncertainty was horrible. I remember the last session we had before the doors shut. We were all very jovial about it all, but there was a realisation that it might be last time we actually train together. That's not an exaggeration. I'm really lucky in that I have great people in my club, and all members of the dojo past and present are genuinely fantastic humans. When lockdown happened, I missed them all.

Six months passed before we got to open the dojo again, but this wasn't the same as the first lockdown. During the first lockdown there was a sense of hope that this would soon be over. It was

121

new and people pulled together, supported each other in a way that felt like a war-time spirit. This time it felt like we'd realised that there was no war, there was no fight, all that was needed was endless patience and nerve. Many didn't seem to have it the second time. It drained people. Jobs were lost, lives were changed, and it felt hopeless. This seemed to translate to the dojo folk. There was less contact than last time. The zoom calls and messages to each other dried up, and there was a sense that at the end of the hiatus there would be no club. The sad thing is that at times I really didn't know whether I cared anymore. The world was changing, and it looked like we had to change with it. I was made redundant at the start of the pandemic, and this really didn't help my mood. I didn't tell many people about it, I didn't think that my burden would improve their moods at all, so what was the point?

During the first lockdown we were invited to a lockdown quiz via a person I'd known a long time from another club. There were going to be lots of other Iaido students from the UK invited, and although I wasn't going to know many of them, I decided to give it a go as it was the closest to a break in the monotony. This turned out to be the best thing I'd ever done for my mental health. I made new friends, some I genuinely treasure, and hope are for life (and if any of you are reading this, I just want to say thank you. I probably can't articulate to you the difference you made to my life during that period, you were brilliant), and I got a quiz to boot. I don't know if, it had not been to this quiz, whether I would have returned to Iaido. The conversations about it in intervals during and after the quiz made it seem new again, and the anecdotes and memories from each person made me realise how much more it was to me than just a hobby. It had become so much a part of my history. The fun of it, the ridiculousness of it, the high and low times I'd had, the raising of glasses to those that had passed with people who I'd shared good times with, and the chance of making more of these memories meant that as soon as this lockdown was over the keys would be in the dojo door, the alarm turned off, and my gi removed from the bag and hung on my shoulders, tighter than before, but ready to go.

When the time came and the hall messaged me asking for RAMS (risk assessments, method statements) to be updated for covid restrictions, I messaged the class on social media and told them we're back on. The response was so enthusiastic. It honestly took 2 months of training to get going again, but we did it with a determination that is to be proud of.

I'd be remiss if I didn't mention my Senpai, or wife as I like to call her, during this period. I'm not easy to put up with at the best of times, as she knows better than anyone, but during the lockdowns she had it the hardest. Working harder than normal to support me, always looking after me and the kids, and always trying to be positive about the situation and how it was going to turn out. I'm a miserable bastard and there were days I'd wake up and not want to get out of bed, but because of her I did, and here we are now with the dojo very much alive, and things are beginning to look a bit like pre-covid. I know it only takes a few bad stats before it could happen again, but I know that with her I'll be just fine. Thank you Mrs.

Iaido words of wisdom: Oshiete kudasai

Means 'teach me please'

This is a nice way of getting the teacher's attention during the lesson when you want to know something.

It's pretty useful when you are training at other dojo and will likely go down better with the Sensei than, 'Oi, I keeping fucking up Kesa-Giri'.

Going to lose one

There are inevitably times when a student stops training permanently.

In the time leading up to the final decision there are indicators that give this away. It's simple to know with YVMs, as they've met someone and instead of training they are shagging for England, and their attendance comes to a grinding halt (grinding being the key word).

With others the process can be a little more gradual. The student misses a session or two, and when they do attend, they over-explain their absence and give a load of excuses (which is interesting as I never ask anyone where they've been. Training isn't mandatory by any means and if you're not coming you don't need a sick note. This isn't school.). Then they miss a few more sessions. When they do attend a practice, they seem tired, not physically, but tired of the whole experience. The enthusiasm is gone, and they don't seem to be enjoying it at all. Then you have the whole fiasco of a month later getting messages saying that they are coming back, it's just that they've got a lot on, or give you some other reasons that seems a bit flaky. Then, ages later, comes one final session: One last denial that the love has died. It's been so long since you've seen them that it's actually a bit of a shock that they've turned up. Then something unfortunate happens. The student notices that the other people there that were of a similar standard have improved and moved on. They notice that they are not as good as they were before, and then on top of that the higher standard that the others have reached now just amplifies it. They have a shit session. Then they disappear, never to be seen again, and no amount of encouragement or solidarity seems to help.

Commitment to any activity is difficult, especially over long periods of time. Life does get in the way of things and sometimes people will start training in Iaido with every intention of doing it forever, and then one day the time comes to get ready for training and you just don't have it in you to go. You think about picking up the bags and going out to the car, but you just can't. Your lai tank is running on empty.

I wish there was a magic formula to motivate myself to do a lot of things, and I've never found it, so I can understand perfectly well why you can get to the point where actually you want to give up. My surprise lies in the journey this takes for the student. Instead of dropping the teacher a line or sending a message saying that they've decided to not continue, so you can end on good terms and leave the door wide open for a return, it fizzles out. The process seems so gradual that the student forgets to let you know they are leaving. Do they still think they're coming back at some point? Have they actually admitted to themselves that it's game over? Are they just embarrassed about it? I don't know. But to date I can only remember one student sending an email to say that they've decided to move on. At least I got to wish someone all the best. There's never bad blood. It just feels empty, after giving so much of your time to someone, for them to slip away unannounced.

Iaido words of wisdom: masters

I once received an email from this chap, claiming to be some martial arts 'master' from a distant land, explaining that he's an expert in every martial art, and as a result of his general superiority (or some such shit like that) can I please send him his 8th dan?

I had to reply properly through the correct channels, and explained that it wasn't possible, and he'd need to train and test like all other students. What I simply wanted to write was:

Nice hat.

The email of destiny

Maybe it's different in a big dojo, but since we're a relatively small outfit I'm always worried about letting a new student walk in through the door without vetting them first. Dojo harmony is everything in a small club and because we have a really tight group, I'm very wary to let anyone in because they will need to fit in well. There are other dojo around so if they won't fit us, the good news is there are others they can try.

When I was a student at another club, they would accept everyone that wanted to come along, and this from time to time included children. I hated this because the usual protocol was that the teacher would palm them onto me or another student in particular so they didn't have to do it. So essentially, we were paying dojo fees to come along and babysit a couple of kids that were trying not to fall asleep as it was getting on for 9pm. To be clear, this is absolutely fine behaviour from the teacher. I was a level 1 qualified teacher and it was their dojo, and it was an acceptable request to make of me. Didn't mean I didn't hate or resent it, I did, but I understood my place. Naturally a month later they'd leave as they were kids, and I was happy when they did. I couldn't also help but notice that when a nutter tried to join, I'd get them for the session also, which is Sensei's prerogative! But because we are small I don't want to accept people that cause issues. If, for example, I have to spend a majority of my time attending to a new student because they're not picking anything up, then the others training will suffer. I could make my seniors look after them whilst I attend to everyone else, but as indicated I didn't like it and I won't do it to them as a result.

The first thing I look at is the initial enquiry about the club. Things that have raised the alarm in the past are emails that have things such as 'I want to learn that ninja shit', or an email address like 'legendarysamurai69@' etc. Fortunately, these are extreme, but I'm not making any of this up.

The other thing I sometimes get is when the dojo enquiry page is filled out and when it gets to me it says something like 'I'm looking to start Kendo, can I join your club?' I'm not sure how anyone is going to cope with the complicated nuances of Iaido when they can't cope with a three-page website that doesn't mention kendo at all. One time I had a phone call from a guy who sounded really out of breath. He said 'man, you gotta teach me Kendo'. I envisioned him on his mobile phone, running away from a bizarre 'Kendo gang' who have beaten him up since he started High School with bamboo swords. I explained that I don't teach Kendo, and he replied 'Yes you do' really aggressively. I apologised but explained that we don't and asked where he'd read that we do? 'It's on your website mate'. So, I asked him to have a look and tell me where? He had a look, and then said, 'You must have taken it off'. What? During the call? Another disappointed customer.

I had a parent message me and ask me to teach his son Kendo. I apologised and said that I don't teach Kendo and I don't teach children, but if he gives me the town they're from I can point him in the direction of somewhere that does that can help him. He wrote back saying please, could I? His son is 13 and very strong and tall. Again, I said I couldn't but if he could just give me the town, I'd be happy to assist him find something suitable. I then got 'Why won't you teach him Kendo'? So, I simply wrote back 'BECAUSE I DON'T TEACH KENDO OR KIDS'. He wrote back

'Kingston upon Thames' (which is, incidentally, fucking miles from here.).

I had a potential student send me a message asking if they could come to a class and give it a try, so I replied and said they could, and added the details of what to wear and bring, and explained how to get a temporary membership from the governing body. They wrote back and said they'd see me at training. Two days later they sent me a message saying that they hadn't slept since our emails having panic attacks about it all, and it was probably best if they didn't come as they were full of anxiety about it. I explained we're a nice bunch and we'd look after them. They still felt that the idea of it was crippling them with fear. It's a shame but it was probably a good idea they didn't come along for everyone involved.

What I guess I'm after is some indicator that the potential student is sensible. An enquiry that's written simply and to the point goes a long way as a starter. 'I'm interested in learning Iaido and wonder if you're currently taking students?' is just perfect. If someone tells me about all the other shit they've done and what grades they are in the opening email, it Shania Twain's me a bit (It don't impress me much). One person listed 9 different martial arts they'd had a go at. All I could think was, bet they're a quitter. It's like giving me a C.V. with all the jobs they'd been sacked from. Their other grades are pretty irrelevant at that stage too.

Once the first email has come through, I send an email back asking the following: Name, age, any medial issues that would cause issues with training, and then the final question: why Iaido?

If I'm going to commit to training a person, I don't think it's too much to have their name, age and list of issues so I don't harm them further. I've had a person before tell me they're not comfortable answering with their age and issues. That's absolutely fine but I wouldn't let them start with us. It's more than me trying to find out about them, it's actually about trust. If someone is willing to answer those pretty simple questions honestly then they've taken the first steps in trusting us, and I'm going to be happier letting them in.

The 'why Iaido' is not a trick question. There's a variety of answers and each seem to give me some idea of what type of student is coming along. If a person says, 'I have done other martial arts and fancy giving it a go', that's great. 'I want to try something different and fancy giving it a go', brilliant. 'I'm into cosplay and want to learn the mighty sword'... well that means there's a chance they're there to dress up and take pictures of themselves, so I at least won't be too surprised if it happens. 'I'm out for vengeance against my school bully'. Sorry, we're full. Whilst I haven't had that as an answer, I once received something that more than implied it. Red alert...

The last student that joined us emailed and said they were interested, they replied to my email with their details and explained that they'd always done martial arts and had recently moved to the area. They were articulate, and they were honest. Brilliant. From the moment they came through the door they fit straight in, just one of the team.

This isn't always the way. Someone comes in and something's just not right. One time we had a new guy and I paired them up with one of my senpai (assistant teacher) for a two-person exercise. Using wooden swords, the idea was for one to make a cut to the senpai's head, and the senpai's job was to deflect the cut. Whilst I was explaining what was going to happen during the exercise the new person patted the senpai on the head and said in a kid's voice, 'I'm going to try and hit you'. The senpai, who could be described as a little grumpy, was totally unimpressed and gave the new person the evil look of death. This didn't seem to deter the new person from doing equally strange things throughout the lesson (which included saying things in falsetto for no reason what-so-ever. I took them to one side and explained that it's probably best not to do things like that, and maybe to try and concentrate on the exercise. I largely did this because when it was their time to swap the senpai might be tempted to smack the shit out of them 'accidentally'. In fact, when it was time to swap, I substituted myself in instead just because I think their patience might have been getting used up. My senpai gave me the look of 'thank god for that' as we swapped over. The new person left after a few weeks, and it was a relief. We all tried hard to make them feel welcome, but eventually when they realised it was hard work, they moved on. That's the thing about Iaido, if you're not fairly mature it's not the martial art for you.

Iaido wisdom of the week: Honne

Means a person's true feelings and desires.

I know what you're thinking; what the fuck has that got to do with iaido?

When you're at a seminar, specifically when they've managed to con a Japanese high grade to come and have their arse kissed by legions of sword swinging wannabies, then it comes into play.

They will tell you your iai is good, when in fact it's dog shit. They know it, but they just won't tell you, even though you would welcome some useful critique. I've heard students saying how pleased they were that thingy Sensei said their kesa giri was nice. Often, you're left scratching your head as to whether the Sensei mistook them for someone else as their kesa giri looked more like the 'introduction to brush strokes'. They're not making it up, it's just honne.

Listen to the advice, listen to the way they describe doing the kata, take everything on board except the praise. It's probably dubious.

The other martial art

On occasion I've been lucky enough to get invited to train at another dojo. It's a really good opportunity to have someone else look at my Iai and give me pointers and help that I wouldn't ordinarily get. It's also usually pretty cheap as the cost of the venue is divided over the attending people, and we get a Nanadan Sensei or two to boot. It doesn't get much better than that.

I lack confidence in these environments. I'm very self-conscious about my Iai, and I really shouldn't be because I'm there to learn like everyone else, but I do find that I don't really show my usual Iai off. The version I show is often small and apologetic as I try to fade into the already small crowd. It's quite sad as the Iai I normally do could be described as big, and whilst not flamboyant it's certainly not apologetic. It's something I really need to work on. I'm shy anyway and when I get to these venues, I usually only know 20 to 30% of the people there, so I tend to go in with my head down, kind of nod to people as they come in, get changed in my corner, then find a bit of floor and warm up trying not to get in people's way. Everyone else seems to know each other better than I do, and they're all hugging and being very sociable. When that happens, I feel like the new kid in school.

It's at these events where sometimes the day is split, and there's an optional session of Jodo in the afternoon. Jodo is a sister martial art to Iaido. It's the art of the short stick (Jo) and I've had exactly three lessons of it in my whole life. The idea of it I think is mostly two-person kata, one with the stick (or Jo), one with the sword (a bokken or wooden sword), and you use the stick to beat the person with the sword (literally at times).

The first time I tried it was on a day's training in a school hall somewhere. I learned the three whole kata I know now at that session (I also think that the word 'know' might be a little too strong. It was more a snog with Jodo than a relationship). The dojo I belonged to was toying with the idea of teaching it at the time as some of the higher grades were proficient in it, so I went out and got myself the stick and a bag, but nothing came of it, so it went in the cupboard.

The next time it came out was one of these training days. They had an odd number of people training so I agreed to join in and give it a go to help out. I explained I knew basically fuck all, but I figured I'd be good enough at the sword bits to at least give someone else an opportunity to get something from the training, and I thought it would be a chance to give it a really good go. They seemed okay with it and off we went.

I was hoping to get the feeling I used to get when I tried a new kata for the first time, but for whatever reason Jodo didn't speak to me in the same way. The teacher on the day, who I'd known for years and didn't really like much, was actually really good at getting the information across and I found a new respect for them, but even they couldn't inspire me. The upside was that if the situation came up again, I knew I'd be able to fit in and give it a go, and also the after- training gathering was really good. Meeting new people, eating a lot of rice, and getting nicely pissed up.

Sometime later that year the opportunity for another one of these training sessions came up. The morning session went okay and

137

then the opportunity for Jodo came up. Again, there was an odd number of people participating, so I said I'd have a go again if people didn't mind me subbing for someone decent. They were kind as usual and partnered me with a lady who I'd met a number of times before and had always been very pleasant to me.

She was clearly very competent at Jodo and was very kind in not picking me up on the all the mistakes I was making and choosing to instead correct the odd one or two howlers I was making. During one of kata, it was my turn to use the jo. The idea of this kata, if I remember correctly, is that as the person with the sword advances and lifts it ready to cut you, you move slightly forward to the right and strike them with the end of the jo directly from your hip, essentially giving them a giant poke to the mid-section. I wasn't doing this correctly, my strike was either too flat or the wrong angle or something, so she was trying to make the adjustments and make it work. A couple of timid goes and she confirmed I was getting it correct, and I felt good, so did another attempt and tried to do it with the speed and effort that she gave to every movement. Unfortunately for me this led to me accidentally striking the lady in a rather sensitive spot (more or less lifting her up) and what followed was the most awkward conversation two sets of eyes can have with each other, hers telling me 'what the fuck man?' and mine giving the most horrified and honest apology in return. Fortunately, she didn't actually say anything to me, instead moving swiftly on to a different subject to spare my blushes. I've never been more grateful to a person for moving on and changing the conversation.

I've not been to any of these events since, largely due to covid, but I think I'll stick to Iai. For everyone's sake.

Iaido wisdom of the week: Otagai ni rei

Means 'bow to each other'.

Heard mostly by me during opening reiho I favour this phrase over the alternative of Kamiza ni rei which means bow to the gods, which is hard for me to stomach, even as a tradition. I get to choose, so ner...

If a high grade is present you may hear 'sensei ni rei' for you to direct your attention to them as a sign of respect, or 'senseigata ni rei' if there is more than one of them.

Since no self-respecting Sensei would visit us, I wouldn't hold your breath on that one.

141

Who are you?

When I trained at my old club, I was often paired off with a guy who was a grade higher than me to do any 2 person drills. I have a lot of respect for this guy as we would often train together away from the club, and he used to give a lot of insight and knowledge to me from his many years of training: he was a student from a young age and although he had gaps of giving up and returning he clearly had an awful lot of passion for Iaido and Kendo (although not for Jodo, he thought it was crap).

There was one session where we were playing with a particular kata, and mucking about with the timing when he asked me what kind of swordsman I am. I had no idea what the fuck he was talking about so naturally I answered, 'fucking amazing, obviously'. He frowned at me and said 'okay, wrong question, I guess. What sort of person are you and what do you think that says about your Iai?' I was confused. What did he mean by that? I just said that I didn't know, and he seemed to drop the line of questioning.

It played on my mind for the next few weeks of training. Had I missed something obvious? I did all the kata the way I'd been shown them, or at least tried to. Replicating what I was shown wasn't ever easy, but that's what I always aspired to. I wanted my Iai to look like my teacher's. I started watching other people doing their kata with this in mind to try and see if I could link what he had asked to the sword work being shown.

I watched him doing Iai one evening. The kata he was practicing is a Koryu (traditional) form. The idea of it is that you're sitting minding your own business when a person to your right goes for their sword, at which point you turn, strike the wrist of your attacker, then draw and place the blade across them, push them to the floor, and cut them to finish them. It's one of my favourites and I practice it often. There was something different about the way he did it though. Something I hadn't really noticed before. The opening attack was quick and strong and comparable to how I try to do it, but once the sword was placed on the opponent he slowed right down, almost savouring the moment, before pushing them down slower than I would, and then the final cut was delivered a second or so after I would do it. So, what did this indicate? The guy was (and is) a truly nice guy, but he is a strong personality. He doesn't suffer fools at all, and I'd seen him in arguments when he was brutal to the person he was arguing with. He's a competitive person and very honest with you when you're not pulling your weight during an exercise. I also think it's fair to say he liked it when people got their comeuppance. So, I asked him is that what he meant?

It was his opinion that you could see a true reflection of someone's personality through their Iai. If you look at the way they do a kata, throughout it there would be indicators that would reveal you as you deal with the situation at hand. Do you deal with the opponents quickly and efficiently without changing your intent, so each cut is the same and each movement under complete control, or would you increase your intensity during the kata at key points showing that you get angry or agitated? Do you cut harder than you should, do you get more aggressive as the kata goes on, over-moving because you're losing control a little? Is your Iai robotic and boring, too slow and completely emotionless? He felt that if you watched these things, it could tell you more about the person than you realise. So where did that leave me? Did he think I was a boring and callow person because of something I do? Did he think I was a brave and fearless person because I go steaming into multiple opponents? What was the diagnosis? He didn't tell me.

I have no idea if this is a known concept or something that he just noticed on his own, but when I watch people I know do Iai I can see their personality traits on show through the kata. Someone I know who is fundamentally lazy does almost apologise to their opponents with their cuts, like they don't actually want to attack them. Another seems constantly angry with life, and they cut like they're constantly angry, using it more like a hammer than a sword. Another is very zen-like, never seeming to be angry with anything at all, and their Iai is the calmest and consistently functional with the cuts always being identical and their movement slow and calculated. The last person to know is always you of course, and I watch my Iai and can't seem to grasp what it says about me. I dare say that I won't be happy to learn whatever it is about myself when I do see it. One day I'll suddenly arrive at the conclusion it says 'wanker' out loud. That'll be a dark and depressing day.

Iaido wisdom of the week: Kiza

Kneeling but up on your toes. So basically the position you make when you lift out of seiza and get your toes under you. I think Kiza might translate as 'the Jenna Jameson position'.

I'm not sure why, so I'd better do some internet research….

That's it.

Mountain or mountains?

I've been examining my standard recently and have been looking at my weaknesses. One of the issues that I work extremely hard on, but never seem to significantly improve, is my footwork. After all these years I still have days where I just plain suck.

I have weird feet. Not the sort of weird feet you see on the internet where there's slight webbing or one really hairy toe, but my feet have always stuck outwards when walking. It's like each foot is 45 degrees out to the sides, and it makes Iaido very difficult for me. Having your feet in a straight line seems to be the indicator for having your hips pointing directly at the opponent. This is not the case for me, as I can walk like Charlie Chaplin and my hips definitely point forward. It's completely unnatural for my feet to point forwards. In doing it, my legs have to turn a few degrees inwards, so when I then bend my legs, my knees move closer together. It means that certain specific parts of a kata can be very difficult. Any time I have to lunge a little and get a bit of distance between my feet my back foot naturally points outwards which is a definite no. I can't sit in tate hiza correctly because I can't turn my foot to sit on it, which is something I've gotten around for years. When I stand up to chiburi (shake the blood off the sword) I sometimes lose balance because I have to stand in a way that I ordinarily wouldn't with the feet forward, and it's uncomfortable and difficult to hold the position. I was hoping that all these years of practicing would have forged my body to do this more easily. It hasn't.

I've spent many hours of my life without a sword walking the katas up and down the dojo, watching my feet. There are days when I'll run through Seitei like this to start the session and warm up, and it looks okay, and then I suddenly revert to looking like a Mr Man character waving a sword about.

I wish I could say I had a plan on how to fix this issue. I don't. All I can really do is keep on pushing forward and try to make it as natural as I possibly can. This is something I've found with Iaido generally. There are things that you can't do correctly yet, and sometimes you never will be able to do them perfectly. When I first trained, I found this very annoying, and it used to really get me down. Now I realise that you have to push on and keep working at it. If you worry about your imperfections to the point that you are frustrated, then you'll never improve. I try to be aware of them and keep chipping away at them, but don't get upset if they're not being corrected quickly. There's always more to learn, more information to take in and more to enjoy, and if you frustrate yourself you'll lose sight of that.

A teacher used to say to me that learning Iaido is like climbing a mountain, and each session you scale a few more feet to get nearer to the top. I prefer to think of it differently, that each challenge in Iai is a different mountain. At the bottom you can't see shit, in fact you can't even see many mountains, but as you get to the top of the first one, you're high enough now to see there are more mountains out there than you realised, and some are even taller. The more you climb, the more you conquer taller mountains, the more you can see that there's to do. You may never climb them all, and you may never get to the top of each one you climb, but as long as you keep climbing, you're going to get better.

Fuck my socks, I'm coming out with all the clichés today.

As I type this, I'm getting ready for tonight's training session. We're currently working on the sitting forms of Seitei as we've got a relatively new student and it's their first time looking at these. I always make it clear to my students that there are those that are better at doing these kata than me out there, and that at times I may even show them something that's not completely accurate even though I'm trying hard to make sure that I am. I think it's important that they realise that your aim is to improve yourself, and that there's no weakness in showing them the bits that I'm striving to improve.

The worst bit for me of any session is demonstrating the kata. In order to put forward something to learn I've got to make it look good enough for them to want to at least aspire to learning it. If it's done badly, they're not going to be inspired much, and will probably wonder why they're bothering in the first place, especially if they can do it to a similar standard themselves. This motivates me to at least try and do my best version of a kata when showing them. However, from time to time something doesn't go exactly right. One time I had a brain fart and showed completely the wrong kata. I'd been thinking about it just before I went to demonstrate a different form, and auto-pilot kicked in and I showed something completely different to the kata I'd been explaining just seconds earlier. I love that the students are all very polite and that no one said anything. Very British. I worked it out on my own very quickly afterwards and I went redder than a chimp's arse. Turns out they all knew I'd fucked up, but just thought I'd get it myself before long and let me continue in my own happy bubble. I was embarrassed but these things happen I suppose.

Iaido Christmas Wisdom: Merry Christmas all.

In the edo period of Japan it was commonplace this time of year for samurai to test cut their katana on Christmas pudding from Iceland (the store, not the country). The hardest of known puddings, if the sharp blade managed to pass through its thick layer of shit fruit the samurai would be confirmed ready by their peers.

If you look at the kata junto carefully, you'll see this in action, and the brandy sauce is carefully cleaned from the blade by your assistant.

Finally, how do you make Iai bread?

Use Iaido...

Lesson Unplanned

In terms of personal development, when I'm teaching a lesson it's naturally very different to when I'm not teaching . It's hard to focus on myself when I've a room of students at different levels, all needing help. I've always found it difficult to pitch a lesson that will benefit everyone in same way. Yes, it's good that everyone tackles basics over and over, as consistency is everything, but when there's a new student in the lesson picking his nose and wondering which is the pointy bit, it's a real artform to get someone who's been training over a decade engaged by the same drills. Everyone needs to be interested, and that includes the teacher. You can get bored with the same old lessons being rolled out, and whilst it's fun to see the new student energised by them, it's good to remember the other students who know those lessons full well. They need something to fill their Iai tanks as well.

When I'm free practicing I try to aim for above 50 kph, that's 50 kata per hour. 60 minutes to knock out 50 decent kata with some thinking time there too and even a bit for a few swigs of overpriced bottled water as I wouldn't trust it from the club's dirt encrusted taps. When I'm teaching, I wonder some days if I even manage to get twenty kata done over a two-hour period. For a martial art that relies on form and repetition that's not anywhere near enough practice. I don't actually know if 50 kph is a good target or not, and I really should ask a high grade at some point, but for me it seems about the right amount of graft an hour to get a decent Iai work-out, and to actually pick some concepts that need working on and give them a proper bit of investigation. Also, it seems the right amount of practice to make my legs ache like a bastard at work the following day. If I don't do that much, then how else would my colleagues hear me wincing all day long getting out of chairs?

Remembering to balance my training with my students' needs continues to be a really tough thing to achieve. When one of them starts to get into something and begins to conquer it I really get invested in it and start pushing them to improve, and at the same time I let my Iai go a bit.

I've tried a number of different things to try and remedy this. One Sensei suggested I play 'follow my leader'. I do a kata; they do the same one. I do another, they copy. This does work, but ultimately, I can only do this when all the students know the kata I'm doing. If someone doesn't know the kata yet then it means I have to revert to only doing the ones they do know, and if their repertoire is small then I'm severely restricted. I tend to roll this type of training out when only Dan graded students are in the room. That way I don't have to explain why I'm stepping backwards to sit down, or why my hands aren't flat against my side, or why I'm cutting lower than normal. There's no benefit to messing up a really junior student my showing things which contradict the rules of Seitei Iai.

If we have more junior students in then I will teach them in the first hour and try to let them free practice the second hour whilst I try and get up to 50 kph, but it seldom works. An hour isn't a lot of time to get a person to learn the details of a kata so that you can leave them alone to do it. What generally happens is that I'll be three kata in and finally uncracking my knees and beginning to warm up again when a question will be asked, and I have to sack the training to explain it to them again. I don't resent the students for doing this. Iaido is a martial art that requires a decent memory, and it's monumentally hard at the start to remember what you've been told in the detail you were told it. It doesn't help my personal training though. I will ask other students to help me out and look after the 'kids', but they'll often be asked a question they don't know the answer to, and once again I'll be pulled away from the blissful peace of free practice to talk about something irrelevant. You do get asked a lot of questions, and maybe one in a hundred is new and something you've not thought about before. Sadly, ninety percent of the questions have obvious answers if they just thought about it for a moment.

I have, on occasion, lied to the students and said that the dojo has closed due to some last-minute reason, and instead had two hours of undisturbed free practice. This usually happens when I've not trained properly in months as gradings have been coming up, or I've had new students taking up all the lesson time, and I feel the need to remember why I practice Iaido at all. An hour in, and I'm back to being the over-excited puppy again, remembering why I love this stupid martial art so much. I get re-energised and can't wait to go back to the club next time and do it all again. Don't get me wrong, I love having students there, and watching their Iai evolve is gold to me, but there is a real place for a silent room, and just you and the smell of clove oil as you practice, and practice, and practice.

The question I question

I was sitting at a table in a bad greasy spoon some time ago with a group of Iaido students, munching down a dirty great breakfast (it would cause me great distress during training later) when the subject of grading paper questions came up.

Favourites that seem to come up a lot are things like: 'name ten parts of a sword', or 'show the footwork from kata number 8', or 'show the angle and height of the cuts from kata number 11', shite like that. We started to discuss them and how they're just too easy to go online and find, and that it was more difficult to go and get stamps to send the questions off than to answer them in the first place. At this point the highest graded of us said that, for their 6th Dan exam, they had to write a paper on 'why Iaido makes you a better person?' Fuck me, that's a step up from 'name two kata from the Shoden set of your school?'

This must be a difficult to question to answer. For starters, what does it mean to be a better person? One person's better is another person's not-so-good. For example, if Iaido made you less aggressive as a person would that be a good thing? At my job that would not be an asset. Less aggressive could mean being far less assertive, and that wouldn't be a benefit to me. Yet being less aggressive can definitely be seen as a positive, especially if a person has a history of violent behaviour.

What if I had trained to a really high level of Iaido, would that have many practical uses in my everyday life, leading to me being a better person? Well, let's examine it. What do I use from the physical teaching of Iaido? Well, I use tora-bashiri (tiger stepping) whenever I go into my kid's rooms at night to turn off

153

lights because it's a really quiet way of walking and I'm desperate not to wake them up. When I'm jogging, I tend to use my tanden (core) to move me forward as I find it's less energy depleting than when I don't use it. Outside of that, can I think of a practical use for anything physical I've learned? Not that I can think of.

Am I more physically fit for practicing Iai than I would be if I didn't? Yes. More than I would be from any other activity? No, not at all. An hour of running over a week would be more beneficial to my body than the equivalent of Iaido. An hour of swimming even more so. But again, the question was 'does it make you a better person' and not 'are you physically better for learning Iaido'.

Then there's the mental side of Iaido. Has there been any change to me mentally? Any benefit to me daily? Well, this one is a little more difficult to answer. It's harder to judge any differences because I don't remember my old self well enough to judge whether it has benefitted me in a positive way. I can't tell if I'm more compassionate now, or whether I'm a better judge of character now, or if I concentrate harder now than I did. What's the control for the experiment? I don't have one.

Because of this I googled 'what makes you a better person' in order to check the results against my experiences with Iaido, and the answers include:

- Being a good listener
- Understanding the other side when you are in conflict
- Anger management techniques
- Determination
- Strength
- Confidence

So, does Iaido affect any of these?

Well, Iaido could possibly help being a good listener. In a lesson you receive a lot of information in a relatively short space of time. You have to listen carefully and assess the information carefully or you can't practice well. When I don't listen attentively, I make more mistakes and occasionally miss the entire point of a lesson, and I've consciously tried to overcome that lack of attention. So, years of listening hard may make you a 'better listener'. That's a box ticked.

Understanding the other side when you are in conflict? Since Iaido is a single person kata-based martial art, I can't see really that there's a whole lot that would help you reach understanding of the other side in an argument. Saying that, being a dojo leader means you have to at times resolve conflicts between students, so that could potentially lead to you having to listen and take on board two peoples opposing views and then make fair or unfair judgements. So, half a tick there, maybe.

Anger management techniques is an interesting category for me to think about. In many ways I find that Iaido **is** an anger management technique, and maybe for me the ultimate anger management technique. The thing I like more than anything is using Iaido as pure escapism from when life is dog-shit, and when I come out of the dojo life feels better than it did, and I can go home and usually are a bit more balanced about things than I was. If I walk into the dojo pissed off and angry it tends to defuse me and calm my shit down. So, there's a strong tick from me.

Determination I don't think is improved by learning Iaido. In my experience a person is motivated, or they aren't. Successful people tend to be very driven and determined and the opposite for less successful people. If you're really driven at being successful at Iaido, you probably already were determined and motivated. It may show your success, but there's probably other things in life you do that would show that. I've been more successful at other things than Iaido, and it certainly hasn't motivated me or fired me up like other things have. There are things that do motivate such as wanting to please a teacher or pass a grading, but that doesn't give you desire, that is the desire, so for me there's no tick. Others may feel differently. Good for them. Aren't different opinions and arguments how we learn?

Then there's strength. Does learning Iaido give you strength? Practice it enough and you will have stronger legs and arms, certainly. Shoulders too. So again, I'd give that a tick.

Does Iaido give you confidence? I'm not sure. I can't say I'm a more confident person for learning Iaido. I was always a gob-shite (hard to believe, isn't it?), and an over-confident one at that, so it's hard for me to say it's been a benefit or not. I watch others and I do find that they grow in confidence, coming into the dojo quietly when they join up, and a few months in really changing and being more outgoing. I'm not so sure that's Iaido increasing their confidence, or just familiarity meaning they've gotten to know the other students better. I've done other activities with a lot more physical contact, and they've definitely given me more confidence than Iaido has, and that has removed much more fear from situations where there is confrontation for me, but Iaido could still build confidence through having to perform kata in front of people, but it's a hard thing to gauge. Potentially it's a yes, but I'd need a lot more proof to give it a solid tick.

156

So, on the google criteria it would appear that Iaido does at least to some extent make you a 'better person', as long as you buy in to those criteria being what makes you 'better'. To what degree you're a better person is up for debate for another time. I don't suppose also that being a 'better person' necessarily means you're a 'good person'. I don't think I'm a good person because of Iaido, or in spite of it (or at all, I don't think I'm good, full stop). If I wanted to be a better person there are much more effective ways of achieving that. If I wanted to be stronger, I'd lift weights and eat protein all day long (we had a student that had to stop every hour to eat boiled eggs, yoghurt or chicken as he was body building. More dedicated than I'd be, he achieved his goal, he looks like musclebound god now, despite eating some seriously boring shit). If I wanted to be more confident, I'd read up on techniques and take classes on how to develop it I suppose. But on the upside, it would seem that Iaido does have other benefits beside the knowledge of how to carve up your opponent like a Thanksgiving turkey. Who'd have thought it?

Iaido wisdom of the week: New student starting Thursday.

I'm hoping he's normal, and isn't the sort of person that wears their trousers up by their neck, or the sort of person that just wants a sword, or the sort of person that makes nunchucks out of a windowsill, or the sort of person that wants to dress as a manga character, or the sort of person that takes their cosplay life a little too seriously, or the sort of person that wants to be a jedi, or the sort of person that thinks the sword has a soul and wants to connect to it.

So, yeah, fingers crossed.

Celebrating the dojo

Every dojo has a get together of some kind here and there. Even as a kid we had a Christmas bash of some variety with too much sugar- and tartrazine-fuelled orange squash. Since running a dojo, I've found it's very important to make time for outside-the-dojo activities.

When we got our first student, we decided to go drinking on a Sunday afternoon after a 5 hour training sesh. He'd been with us about 3 months and frankly we hardly knew him, so suggested a couple of drinks at the pub hoping to learn more about him. What followed was 4 straight hours of hardcore drinking of whisky, beer and wine. He was doing very well, keeping up with my wife who had alcohol running through her veins that day, and we realised we had a kindred spirit, right up until the moment he pointed out that he actually doesn't really drink, and that he'd really enjoyed the evening, but was now completely fucked. Astonished, we watched him hug the wall on the way to the toilet in the hope that it would stop the room spinning. He did really rather well. He didn't fall on his face. There wasn't any bone breakage. Respect to him. A couple of months later he came over for dinner and brought a bottle of Sailor Jerry's for me to enjoy. He and my wife again got utterly destroyed on the rum and in fact downed the lot. I went to bring out the dessert and found them both on the carpet, sitting in tate hiza, trying not to fall on their faces, giggling like children. Another successful excursion for my student.

Several years later we decided to have the first dojo barbeque. I'm a bit of an amateur chef and enjoy putting out ridiculous banquet sized barbeques, so I would cook whole animals on the coals and serve them on slabs of wood with carving knives so people can help themselves, we filled up a dustbin full of ice and beers and sat in the garden getting smashed on a beautiful summer's day. There's so much more to the guys than wearing giant strides and waving swords about. Chewing the cud with them is one of my favourite things. Nothing beats playing Exploding kittens with a bunch of pissed people whilst hearing about the time they caught their bollocks on a see-saw when pissed at the park.

One of the students who had been with us a while ate solidly from 1pm to midnight; I mean the guy literally had food in his hand or on a plate the entire day, pausing only to drink even more. In fact, in order to make the journey home we filled him a box full of meat. He was grateful. It was apparently gone at the end of the 30-minute journey. His toilet must have cried itself to sleep the next day.

Christmas parties are the most common dojo excursions. I've been to at least one at every club I've belonged to. I went to a Mexican restaurant for one of them and got sat next to the most boring person I've ever sat with. I tried to engage them in conversation, but they were too busy moaning about the fact their spiced tuna was too spicy, which made me drink more Modelo beer than I ever thought possible. Iaido might make you a better person but fuck me that doesn't guarantee you'll be a more interesting one. I can talk bollocks with anyone, as long as they've got a personality. This chap didn't have one fitted as standard.

Our first dojo crimbo bash was awesome. All the students and their other halves came, and we gave plastic katanas filled with jelly beans to each of them. Nothing beats a yoko chiburi (side blood flick) when you can lob jellybeans into another students mouth. Admittedly the other people in the restaurant were annoyed that we didn't provide them with children's plastic jellybean swords. Who wouldn't be? A sword AND sweets? Shit doesn't get much better than that.

I tried to do a proper Hatsugeiko (first training of the year) a few times, but they've never worked out as planned. The idea each time was to have a chilled practice, then get everyone to do an embu, followed by a cup of hot sake to toast the year, then down the pub to toast it a whole lot more. One year one of the students brought the bottle of sake which I thought was really nice. Sadly, though as he got out of the car he stumbled and accidently spiked the bottle on the ground, shattering it into tiny pieces. No one was more devastated than him, as he was quite a fan of alcohol, and the only real shock was that he didn't drop to his knees and mouth-vacuum the liquid off the pavement. Another year I accidentally left the dojo keys at home. I arrived with everyone ready to go and do their thing at the dojo, but instead ended up buying everyone dinner at the pub as it was totally my fault. Bugger.

Iaido wisdom of the week: Suburi

Suburi refers to practice cutting. That shit I make you do at the start of lessons cutting to chin and waist? Suburi.

There are various types, some one-handed, which is ideal for knackering your arm prior to training, alternating cuts to the left and right of the head, ones with different step combinations, all sorts.

What's important is that you're practicing each cut fully and properly, and not just waving the sword about, or using it to cut like a sledge-hammer. Don't practice bad habits because if you do you'll likely just bed in bad habits which will be harder to get rid of later. Yes, you may end up with guns Arnie will be proud of, but the chances are your cutting skills will either resemble a man demolishing a patio, or a 99-year-old fisherman casting off.

Good lord

Years ago, we were using a different hall to the one we are in now. It was a much bigger venue, but the floor was a bag of shite which is why we ultimately moved away. It was a church hall and as such was located behind a pretty large church, and some days parking got a little bit interesting as parishioners don't always seem make the best car parkers. Often, I would pull in, and because I was using the hall and not the church itself, they seemed quite happy to make me wait whilst they conducted a 39 point turn to leave a space you could just get out of really easily, putting their head down in shame as they eventually went past me.

I used to get changed in the kitchen as it was the only room apart from the main hall not covered in spiders, and also I could keep an eye on my car as the church kicked out. That was a good use for the room as we were never going to use it as a kitchen, and it was big, and contractually we had an agreement that during our training hours we were the only people allowed in the venue and had full use of the facilities. Before going into the hall, I would lock the front door. I've been training a few times over the years when drunk people come in to see what you're doing on a Friday night, and I can't be arsed with the hassle.

One evening it was just me and the Mrs. We arrived at the hall and there was a full-on chorus coming from the church next door. The usual combination of terrible singing and badly parked cars meant there was apparently a well-attended service happening. We got changed and I locked up the front door just in case somebody decided they wanted to come in, before going into the hall. We started warming up and stretching and decided we would work on a particular kata that involved a lot of cuts, one after the other, as you travel forward.

We heard the sound of people creeping into the building, and shortly after the sound of running water and the noise of a tea urn being switched on. I didn't care because as long as they were quiet, I didn't mind them being there, even though they shouldn't have been.

The noise began to grow to a point where training was getting a bit difficult. She couldn't hear what I was saying, and I was starting to get fed up, so I decided to have a chat with them. I took my sword out of my belt, placed it to the side of the hall, put my flip flops on, and wandered into the kitchen. As I did the room fell silent. 15 or 16 older ladies, all armed with tea. I said, 'excuse me everyone, you're not meant to be here and you're making a lot of noise and I'm trying to train my student, would you mind keeping the noise down please?' There was a sort of nod of agreement. A 6 ft 2 man dressed in Japanese clothing stood before them sternly asking them to shut the fuck up (but politely). They didn't know what to do, but their faces showed that they were not happy at being told they couldn't natter loudly. This was THEIR turf, and I, despite paying, was not welcome right now as I was interrupting their parish social life. I nodded in a sort of half bow, and said, 'and please, whatever you do stay out of the hall' and retreated back to my student.

Training continued and the noise fortunately had died down significantly, although I could feel tension, like something was wrong, but despite that I continued on.

We heard the front door go and whispers happening, but I assumed it was just people going home and the remaining god-botherers keeping it down finally. At last, peace. So, I asked my Mrs to show me where she was at with the kata. She drew the sword and began cutting. Cut to chin, move and cut to sternum, move and cut to waist, move and crosscut, move and... It was at this exact moment that a Vicar, who it turns out the ladies had summoned to 'have a word with me', decided to open the door and come bowling in. He obviously felt very confident and went to stride into the hall, only he it did as my wife launched her final cut, and it landed 3 inches in front of his belly. A split second sooner and he quite possibly would have been on his way to heaven a little sooner than he predicted. He stood there frozen, white as a sheep, mouth open, stunned. Impressively she continued the kata by performing the blood shake before putting the sword back in the scabbard. As she began to slowly retreat, I looked at him with my death stare, and said, 'Yes?' He swallowed hard and said, 'Er, can I use the toilet?' Now I'm not saying that the near miss cut had changed his mind about coming in to see us for a 'chat', but there were toilets next to the corridor he was in. I just think he wanted to change his underwear. Behind him the gaggle of ladies looked in through the door, mortified.

3 minutes later the building was suddenly clear. I heard him say 'we'd better leave now' to them, and they followed him out the door like a religious conga. Then there was finally peace. The sort of peace you can only get by nearly twatting the local vicar.

Iaido wisdom of the week: Seme

Seme (pronounced sem-may). Not Semi, as in 'she was sort of hot, she gave me a semi'.

Seme means the unrelenting pressuring on the opponent by attacking.

There are different types of seme:

Ken o Korosu: Kill their sword (move the opponent's sword out of center to attack).

Waza o Korosu: Kill their technique (you can do this with a block/ or stop/ or counter (Uke Nagashi).

Ki o Korosu: Kill their spirit (Kiai, or simply overpowering them with force or good timing).

Ken O Streetfighter Korosu: Kill your opponent with hadouken.

The after-grading deflation

When I passed a grading last, I had that euphoric feeling you get. I trained hard to pass the grading. I spent months showing my Iai and getting feedback, then I'd work tirelessly on that feedback, then show my Iai again, be told the exact same feedback as before, go away and work on it again, and then hope that next time I show my standard that I've actually improved.

I've never been good at changing subtle movements quickly. If I need to make an improvement it can take me a really long time to get to doing it consistently. I understand the information I'm getting, but changing it so that every time I do it, I remember it is something I struggle to master. It's more than repetition, it's remembering to change it each time I practice it so that it becomes useful repetition. I have to really concentrate on that change one painful kata at a time. Nothing comes naturally or easily to me. Constant concentration on specific kata over months meant that eventually I got the piece of paper at the end of the test.

I came back to the dojo and the first lesson was great. I stood slightly further up the line as I'd gone up a grade: the reward for the hard work. I had applause at the end of the class as the teacher announced my pass. Some of the students didn't like me but had to clap along. That felt good: knowing they didn't like me but had to clap me. Was almost worth it for them to have that indignity.

Then the next week came, and I felt empty. The next grading seemed so very far away. I couldn't take it for years. I couldn't motivate myself to throw myself back into the preparation with the intensity that I'd had before.

The next few weeks were more of the same. There was one night where I spent more time concentrating on watching the yoga class next door than on my Iai. Not in a pervy 'I like a sweaty leotard' way, but in the movements. It was at least new and interesting, and not more of the same movement I'd had each and every week.

I joined in with lessons as I always had, but we seemed to be going over the same old things, the vast majority of which I'd just spent a year focusing on. I realised I was getting bored. Timing wasn't good too, I was having other life problems and not having the grading to concentrate on meant I couldn't distract myself in the same way that I had previously. I really hated being at home, I really hated being at work too, and suddenly I realised I was beginning to dislike Iaido, when it was the one thing that made life bearable. Well, that and pornhub, but mostly Iaido.

I went to class one day and was at a real low. I was trying to follow on with the class, but it wasn't going well. I wasn't in the mood. I lacked motivation and I seriously lacked fighting spirit. My cuts were flopping about a flaccid cock, and my movements were plodding and robotic. The class wasn't being taken by Sensei that night, but instead was being taken by his senior student who noticed my apparent shit-ness, and he asked me if I was okay. Ordinarily I would have been very respectful and probably just made something up and said I'd try harder, but instead I told the truth. I explained that since the grading I was de-motivated and not enjoying Iai.

I didn't want to offend him. I actually enjoyed his teaching as much as I enjoyed Sensei's. He made lessons interesting and different, which was always welcomed by me. I wanted to make sure he realised that he wasn't the problem was, and that it was purely me and my attitude that was the issue. Fortunately for me he had felt similar feeling before after he had passed a grading. He suggested I use the time wisely and take a year off from 'training for the grading' and instead work on the more advanced techniques purely for fun. I knew them all to a very basic level, and had spent a few lessons here and there going over them, but never practiced them for long, and the idea of actually spending a lot of time on them to really give them a good innings was an intriguing idea. A year of Koryu.

What followed was one of my favourite years of study.

I started with Shoden, which is the first level of Koryu, and spent 5 months solidly working on the forms and reading everything I could about them. I started off by trying to break each of them down into a very basic 'foot goes here, cut goes here' way of doing them. Once I could complete each movement and felt I had decent posture and stability for each I then moved on to smoothing them out a little. I have video of various teachers doing them and would try and mimic the way they performed the kata, in particular copying the speed and timing. Often, they would do them in a way I'd never considered and I really enjoyed this aspect of training. I had to re-evaluate the bunkai (situation happening within the forms) and consider greater details of what was happening. This was a bit of a revelation.

169

Changing my Iaido to be like theirs is, of course, a challenge and the final result would obviously not be the same, as I couldn't do them as well as they could, but I could definitely see development happening with each form. Suddenly I was back and interested again. I got that thrill again of wanting of come along to training and finding something new to fill my Iai tank. This continued as I gave each set a really good going over. Each time I looked at something new I got that throbbing feeling in my Iai sausage. Iaido started being the cathartic experience it had been to me for so many years before, and once again training began to be my relief from the world. Then something unexpected happened. At the point where I went back to looking at Seitei Iai again in detail I found it far more interesting and inspiring than I had ever before. It had been a long time and I hadn't practiced them hardly at all. Each was like a new form, and I started looking at them again as if this was the first time I'd ever approached them, going through them in the same detail as I had the Koryu, starting with the basics of my feet and stability, and moving through the forms by looking at all aspects of them.

If you're ever finding that Iaido isn't rubbing your rhubarb as once it was then I recommend trying this, or at least something similar. Not all development needs to be grading based. Sometimes all you need is the spark to ignite something that'll really grasp your attention, and then run with it.

Iaido wisdom of the week: Chakuso

Refers to the manner of how you wear your Gi, Obi, Hakama, and sword.

For me the most annoying thing you see in Iaido is when someone is displaying a fuck-load of chest beard because their Gi is open. It's lazy, and it's not a nice sight. You're learning Iaido, you're not David Hasslehoff in Knight Rider. I don't need to see the chest equivalent of a builder's bum.

In terms of Chakuso this is more significant than a shit fashion choice. It's showing that your attitude is lazy, because you can't be arsed to dress yourself properly you probably can't be arsed with your training as a whole. It's an indicator that you're not taking things seriously.

There are other indicators too. The sword not sitting properly because you haven't tied your Obi or Hakama correctly is another indicator that you might not be trying too hard as apparently dressing yourself was a bit much today.

Make sure your Gi isn't too large or (worse) too small. Put your Gi on properly so that you are covered to your neck and tie your belt well so that the Gi stays there. Hakama on and again tie it well so that everything stays where you want it to. I tend to pull the belt reasonably tight before tying it up, and then tie the hakama more firmly as I find it supports the saya well, whilst still giving me ease of movement for Sayabiki. Too tight and the fucker won't move. Too loose and it flops around during your kata like a freshly caught salmon.

171

Peter Cetera should write a song about that

One of the interesting things for me with Iaido is who I look up to and admire. The people that inspire me in the Iai world are varied and it's not always for the obvious reasons. Grade alone is great and all, but it takes more to inspire me to learn or try harder. There's always more than Iaido to see.

I was once at a weekend training day when the Japanese Sensei were teaching. They don't teach at every event, in fact it's pretty rare, especially in modern covid times, and this was a really good opportunity to get the information at the source, instead of learning it from others passed down. There were six Rokkudan (6th Dan students) on the floor that day being used to demonstrate the kata. The format was simple enough: a quick explanation and translation of the Kata, then a demonstration by the sixth Dan's of the kata, followed by that demonstration being absolutely ripped apart by the Japanese Sensei who, in front of everyone, corrected every error, made conspicuous every flaw, and pushed them hard to do better.

It was tough going for each of them, and I honestly felt bad for them. I don't like being centre of attention particularly, even for positive things I've done, so this would be utterly mortifying for me. However, it wasn't like this for several of these people. Four of the six noticeably lapped this teaching up, taking it on the chin and were really trying to correct the mistakes, not being phased by it one bit. No embarrassment or pained faces, just gratitude and positive attitude.

Several years on I can say I know three of these people (to me, teachers) reasonably well and have been lucky enough to have

172

received a lot of teaching from two of them in particular. My first impression of them never changed. They are total whores for Iai information, and they just continue to get better and better. On top of this they're also bloody nice people, and when it comes to being inspired, I look to that first moment. I often tell my students of what I saw that day, and how important that message is. If you get scrutinised and are told you're not doing it right you can get the arse and blame everyone, or you can follow that example, take it in your stride, and do it better.

Not all inspiring people in Iaido are top level high-grade students. I once had a guy message me about starting at the club. He was a Hungarian chap who was looking at giving Iaido a go, and so along he came to see if it was something he wished to pursue. He was an extremely quiet person. His English was excellent, and he was clearly well educated and although I can't remember his occupation I do remember being impressed by it. I had real concerns as to whether we'd be a good fit for him because he was so introverted, and frankly we weren't. He'd come along, get changed, take the floor and work very hard. He'd listen to every instruction and was a complete natural, to the point that I wondered if he was hustling us and that he was in fact a long term student of the art. To date he's the most naturally talented beginner I've known.

I asked him one day if we were 'okay' for him, and whether he enjoyed it or not? He was so quiet I really wanted to make sure he wasn't feeling overwhelmed or intimidated by us, and that he was actually getting something from it, especially as he'd been with us a little while now. He piped up and explained that since he joined us it was the first time he'd felt accepted anywhere since coming to England, whether at work or outside, and that he really liked just being one of the guys. It suddenly occurred to me just how difficult it must be to walk into a place like ours, and try to fit in, especially coming from a different country. I had so much respect for the guy anyway, but so did all the other students at the club, and it wasn't too long before he was as chatty and irreverent as all the other guys, coming right out of his shell. He even once told us his best accidental poo story, which naturally gets you kudos in our club.

Iaido seems to attract a lot of creative and artistic people, but for me one stands head and shoulders above the others. In my house I have a huge print from an amateur photographer who also happened to once be one of my teachers. I absolutely love his photography, seriously it's fucking fantastic. He can turn the most mundane and ordinary view and turn it into something that turns your head. If I'm taking a picture, I genuinely try to emulate his style, with absolutely no success. The only way I'm going to ever have an artistic bone in my body is if Banksy shags me. It also doesn't hurt though that he has really honest Iai. It's an elegant style of Iaido that looks really simple (and Iai isn't at all simple) that I've also tried to emulate with similar lack of success. Still, I'm not giving up.

One of my absolute inspirations is a man that has essentially reached the pinnacle of Kendo, Iaido, and the other stick one. He has probably forgotten more than I'll ever know about Iaido, and if you're lucky enough to practice under him at training weekends then you're in for a treat as you will hear explanations and advice that will seriously elevate your skills. I was once being taught by another teacher who was struggling to convey something, so he called this person over and asked if he could help. Two sentences later and we were all doing it correctly. As he walked off the teacher turned to us and said, 'That's why he's the best there is'. Whilst I don't disagree one bit with that teacher's sentiment, that's not why I'm so inspired by this person. I look up to them because despite sitting at the top of the Iai food chain they don't appear to take it all that seriously. Don't get me wrong, they are obviously completely committed to it and love it, but they seem to be able to see it for what it is, and within that enjoy it. And on top of this: my god he is fucking funny. I don't just go to these weekenders for training, I go because I know I'm going to learn and be entertained. Beyond this though I'm not sure Iaido would exist in the UK without his contributions both to the art and the governing body.

Speaking of which, when you work alongside people in trying to make an organisation good for everyone you often meet people that give their time for the good of the association for no actual benefit to them at all. There is a lady in the association that has done this for years and years, giving free legal advice, contributing to many areas that meant they could all develop to benefit everyone, from child protection to health and safety: those things that people that join the organisation take for granted. I'm always inspired by people that give without needing to receive and she's the consummate example of this. On top of this she's a fucking diamond of a person.

The truth is there are so many more I could mention from people I've met on Saturday nights at seminars to people at AGMs to of course my wife who obviously inspires me daily.

I hope that I can inspire someone in the Iaido world someday like those people have me.

Iaido wisdom of the week is: In-yo

The Japanese pronunciation of yin-yang, the unity or complimentary of opposites.

Throughout kata, from the serenity of the initial step that is not aggressive, to the draw and aggressive attack, before returning to the harmony of the sword being back in the Saya. It's the transitioning between the two states.

Think about the pain before a difficult fart, then the relief after a difficult fart is passed. Then misery at an unexpected follow through.

In-yo.

Iaido, Poutine and being respectful

So recently I went on holiday to Canada, specifically Montreal, for reasons that had nothing to do with Iaido and plenty to do with me eating vast quantities of smoked meat and sucking down gallons of overpriced beer.

We went out walking on the first day and made our way through the streets which were unsurprisingly empty as jet lag had fucked us up completely and it was 5.45am. It's quite nerve-racking walking through a completely new to you town in a new to you country. What's the etiquette? What are the do's and don'ts? The first frightener of all things was crossing the road. There are no cars coming at all, but people wait until the white okay to walk sign comes on, and sometimes this takes ages. Can you just walk when it's completely safe, or will a huge police officer put down his bagel and poutine, race over and cuff you face down on the pavement? I mean sidewalk. Whatever.

It was on this journey we came across something very familiar: an Iaido dojo. From the outside it looked suitably over the top, with Japanese decor and a lot of wood everywhere, and tatame mats taped together inside. So, we thought bugger it, when it's open, we'll go along and watch the class.

A friend of mine warned me against doing this. He explained that the style of Iaido we would see would likely be very different to what I train in, but despite this I still fancied watching a class. A stranger in town and the familiarity of an Iaido dojo was hard to resist.

We opened the dojo door and slowly crept in. Most of the students were already kneeling on the mat, and all seemed restless as soon as we walked in. A guy came over and asked if he could help. We explained we'd like to watch and, looking confused he asked why? We explained we're Iaido students and fancied watching. He said okay and showed us to some seats and we silently sat as the class began.

The teacher, dressed in Aikido garb with a hakama thrown over the top stood at the front of the class. His hakama was tied messily and he had a serious amount of unnecessary chest beardage on show. He then led the class though the most unusual warm up I've ever seen. Everyone waived the swords around in every direction for a good ten minutes. It must have done a lot for the cardio of the student, and sweet fuck all for improving technique. None the less it had a sort of quality I felt I might be able to 'borrow' for my class, just making sure my students actually do it in a more constructive way.

This as it turned out was the high point of the class.

I can be a proper twat sometimes. A lot of the time, really. But when we watched the class I really had to have a word with myself. I went with the sole idea of enjoying seeing a class in action, and no matter the standard I wanted to come away with something positive, whether it be a way of doing a technique, or whatever. Just something that made it worth the time. However, when I was in there, I just had ego overload inside my head, judging all of the iaido I was watching, and trying to not to smirk. You see the iaido was very basic. It was actually the same style as ours but done really badly. Really, really badly. Feet everywhere, bad technique, poor cuts, no pressuring or attacking, in essence it was more like watching people dance about a bit with swords, and none of those swords would ever bother an opponent. The worst candidate for this? The teacher. He was sloppier than a sloppy joe, covered in olive oil and a can of Castrol.

Every time the class turned away my wife and I exchanged brief glances that said more than we could communicate in a string of texts. Still, we remained quiet and observant. Thing is though, it was difficult. We have spent many years learning and examining and working on improving our style of Iaido. Here was someone doing a toilet on it. Unintentionally maybe, as for all I know in his school his Iai is considered the bollocks. For me it was just bollocks.

The teacher approached me and said hello. He was a friendly chap and seemed happy enough to have us there, and I wasn't going to be an arse in his dojo and say anything negative at all. It's his house, not mine. Still, my mind screams sometimes and as I was making polite conversation, I could hear my inner self shouting out tonnes of 'helpful' advice that I couldn't possibly say. I'm also used to learning Iaido in an environment where if you're doing something shit then someone should have confidence to tell you. How else do you learn? I encourage that in my club.

When the class finished, we got up, bowed, and bowed out. I had a nice chat with the senpai who assumed I was Australian from the accent and asked if he could train at ours if ever in the UK, and I said of course. It'll never happen. I'm kind of glad.

When we walked out the door it was a good hundred metres before we burst and discussed everything we saw. The good news is that it wasn't all bad, and I'm glad we did it. It's made me realise too that I need to be a bit more open minded of the different styles and ideas of Iaido. Sometimes I should just enjoy it.

They were.

Under the hakama

The first time I attempted a seated kata in Iaido I discovered that there is more to think about than knee pads, clearing your hakama out the way, and where to look.

As I started to descend, my boxer shorts started to rise, grasping a testicle on the way up. I winced in pain as it then continued to throttle the poor sod like a scene from a gangster film. This continued all night throughout training, causing me to slip my hand inside the gap and have a corrective rummage of my crown jewels, which as I discovered you can't really do as nonchalantly as you would like to. This was going to be a problem. People did not need to see playing with my Davina McCall's in-between kata. What was I going to do?

First, I thought I'd try the cheapest option and go commando. My thought process was simple. Maximum freedom, minimum pain, as there would be no possibility of snagging. I went along to training and realised that getting changed with everyone else was going to be challenge. This wasn't a swimming pool changing rooms. People did not need to see my over-sized milky white arse or even worse my love spuds or candy rock in the kitchen of the local community hall as they got ready. I had to shuffle off to the toilets which I'm sure gave everyone the impression that I was exceedingly body conscious. I wasn't, I was simply protecting them from seeing their dinners again.

I don't know if going commando works for others, but it didn't work for me. Every time that I knelt down, the hakama brushed against my helmet in long and unnecessary strokes to the point that I didn't know whether I'd get a rash or an erection. Neither would be welcome, especially the latter during training. This was not going to be the solution.

I went to the underwear capital of the UK, Marks and Spencers, and navigated their men's under-crackers looking for something tasteful to wear that would do the trick. I purchased a pack of 5 pairs of 'trunks'. These were smaller than my usual big ol' boxers and looked like they might keep things a little more contained whilst giving me the protection I needed. Also, in the changing room I wouldn't look too ridiculous. Training came and I strode out with confidence that this was the answer to my problems.

A couple of seated forms in and things felt okay. Great. This was going to be a win at last.

It was halfway through the lesson when I dropped to my left knee and was hit with a pain I'd not felt very often in my life. Turns out I twisted my left bean during the manoeuvre. Not good. Fortunately, I managed to reverse the damage with a little help from a soft handed doctor the following day who was perfectly okay with listening to me swearing during the procedure.

Another trip to Marks and Spencer followed. This time I decided to drop the desire for a decent aesthetic and went all out on the need for protection. Yes, I purchased the smallest briefs I could find.

I can't explain the look when I slip into a pair of these. Think 'brit abroad' by a swimming pool and you get the image of just how bad it is of a look. I mean it's maximum security, you can't beat that. There's no chance of anything moving or getting caught. It's like a harness for the scrotum.

Years later these are still my favoured variety. I still look like pervert wearing them. I still hide away in the corner to get changed, and of course I still repulse my wife on occasion by doing a sexy dance in them, but I can happily say that every time I have taken seiza since putting a pair on I've had no issues whatsoever, and everything has been stowed away where it should be.

Iaido Wisdom of the week: Taikai

Taikai refers to competition or tournaments.

Iaido tournaments are not really my bag. I find them stuffy and long and as I have the attention span of a 3-year-old. I don't have the patience for them. You have to wait around a lot whilst everyone gets organised and it's just a waste of a day, especially if it's a hot day. A hot day in a sweaty hall with lots of Iaido folk smelling of feet and arse, or a day on a British beach eating ice cream and avoiding broken glass? Mine's a Cornetto.

Competitions are fairly simple. Usually, you all do three prescribed forms. Do better than your opponent and flags are raised for your side. Do worse, and they go the other way. Both do the same and naturally it will be decided on other things such as who pushed in front of the high grade in the lunch line, or who helped set up at the start, or who has bigger breasts. Or something Iai-related. Maybe.

I do suggest having a go at competition at least once or twice. You get to meet other Iai folk, and you do get to see some really good quality Iai from those that do give a toss about it. You might win a bit of flimsy plastic too if you're good on the day. How about that, eh?

In the afternoon there's a team event where you get to compete with two other people in a group against other three-person teams. There's strategy involved in this. Do you put your best person first or last for example? The order can have a significant effect on the results. When you see the kata that will be performed do you order depending on who has the hot hand with those particular forms? All can change the results.

Onwards and upwards

So, I'm back to trying to build the dojo up after covid has shaved off a few students and there's a bit of room available. We have a website that tells me when someone is looking at it, and roughly where they are geographically, and it gives me lots of stats as to what page has been looked at, and for how long. We're getting more traffic as the weeks pass and covid slips down the headlines, so hopefully it won't be long before we're full again, although I do actually prefer the dojo when there's less people as training is more personal and I don't have to teach to accommodate all levels. Financially I prefer it to be full as it means the bills get paid without us having to subsidise it ourselves. Running a dojo isn't cheap, you know.

I like the website as it'll send me a foreign location of someone browsing it just minutes before someone attempts to scam me. It's great for heading off shit nice and early. The other day I had a request to join our club come through from Brazil. I'm not sure that's going to work for weekly training. They're going to be royally fucked off when they see how bad the public transport is round these parts.

Onwards and upwards

So I'm back to trying to build the dojo up after covid has shaved off a few students and there's a bit of room available. We have a website that tells me when someone is looking at it, and roughly where they are geographically, and it gives me lots of stats as to what page has been looked at, and for how long. We're getting more traffic as the weeks pass and covid becomes less the current news story, so hopefully it won't be long before we're full again, although I do actually prefer the dojo when there's less people as training is more personal and I don't have to teach to accommodate all levels. Financially I prefer it to be full as it means the bills get paid without us having to subsidise it ourselves. Running a dojo isn't cheap you know.

I like the website as it'll send me a foreign location of someone browsing it just minutes before someone attempts to scam me. It's great for heading off shit nice and early. The other day I had a request to join our club come through from Brazil. I'm not sure that's going to work for weekly training. They're going to be royally fucked off when they see how bad the public transport is round these parts.

So, the book is coming to an end and I'm trying to think of a decent ending, which isn't easy considering the format of the book which is mostly me musing about all things Iaido in my life and wanting to convey the enjoyment and the misery. There's no big finish or reveal, no shock conclusion or twist, but in some respects that is what Iaido is like. There's no secret formula to success (assuming that getting better at it is what you deem as success), there's no big finish, there's just the simple formula that what you put in is what you get out. Good old hard work prevails.

What I've tried to really get across is the passion I have for this utter madness. Like lots of hobbies and activities Iaido can burn deep into you and can affect you in a way that other things simply don't seem to. There really is nothing I like more than picking up the bags and heading on down to the dojo, seeing some good people, working really hard on technique and having a great de-stressing few hours before moving on to gutter conversation and discussion of breasts. Iaido is the catalyst for me to have a better life.

So, all that leaves me to say is domo for reading this book.

Cheers, ears.